KT-418-860

psychometric tests

What the best candidates know, do and say

Robert Edenborough

Harlow, England • London • New York • Boston • San Francisco • Toronto • Sydney • Singapore • Hong Kong
Tokyo • Seoul • Taipei • New Delhi • Cape Town • Madrid • Mexico City • Amsterdam • Munich • Paris • Milan

PEARSON EDUCATION LIMITED

Edinburgh Gate
Harlow CM20 2JE
Tel: +44 (0)1279 623623
Fax: +44 (0)1279 431059
Website: www.pearsoned.co.uk

First published in Great Britain in 2009

© Pearson Education 2009

The right of Robert Edenborough to be identified as author of this work has been
asserted by him in accordance with the Copyright, Designs and Patents Act 1988.

ISBN: 978-0-273-72346-2

British Library Cataloguing-in-Publication Data
A catalogue record for this book is available from the British Library

Library of Congress Cataloging-in-Publication Data
A catalog record for this book is available from the British Library

The publishers would like to thank SHL Group Limited for permission to
reproduce Appendix 2, a sample report from SHL Group Limited, 2008.

10 9 8 7 6 5 4 3 2 1
13 12 11 10 09

Typeset in 10/14pt Plantin by 30
Printed and bound in Great Britain by Henry Ling Ltd., at the Dorset Press,
Dorchester, Dorset

The publisher's policy

Contents

Preface

A lot has been written about psychometrics, much of it with the intention of helping candidates understand the types of items they will face in undertaking psychometric tests. This book shares that intention with the aim of giving candidates a broader feel for the entire setting in which tests are used and helping them relate to that setting, for instance in thinking about how to conduct themselves when receiving feedback on tests. As a test user and one who advises clients on the results of tests, I have often been struck by some of the misconceptions that candidates hold and how they sometimes fail to see the testing process in the round as part of selection or recruitment.

I also thought it important to set out some of the individual assessment methods likely to be encountered by candidates that go beyond tests as most commonly understood. Many of these procedures – from structured interviews to in-baskets and self-screening questionnaires – share the characteristics of tests 'proper'. They will often be encountered in company with the more familiar ability and personality measures and I believe that candidates would do well to anticipate their use.

Altogether I hope this book will help candidates to put their best foot forward whatever part of the spectrum of psychometrics they encounter.

Robert Edenborough, March 2009

About the author

Dr Robert Edenborough is a chartered occupational psychologist who has spent most of his lengthy career in the business of assessing people in connection with their career choices. In 2007 he co-founded Bradenlaw Ltd, a company providing reviews of assessment methods and direct assessment support to employers. He has used psychometric tests extensively in his work, which has ranged from candidate evaluation in connection with recruitment to development and helping individuals understand their potential. He has written three books on assessment methods from the point of view of the users of psychometric tests and other approaches. In *Brilliant Psychometric Tests* he directs his attention to the candidate, exploring the experience of undertaking psychometric tests. He provides numerous practical tips on what to do and what not to do, whether someone is facing a single 20-minute test online or evaluation at a two-day assessment centre.

Acknowledgements

I am grateful to Wendy Lord of Hogrefe for bringing the opportunity of writing this book to my attention and for a number of ideas on recent developments in testing. Jackie Switzer and Caroline Milton at Rockpools provided helpful input based on their experiences in the application of tests. David Rogers of Bradenlaw supplied input based on his use of the 16PF and NEO instruments. My wife, Marion, gave encouragement throughout writing, as well as reading and commenting on the text. I also owe a considerable debt of gratitude to the many thousands of candidates and other participants who have gone through psychometrics with me over the last 45 years and whose reactions and comments have helped form such insights as I have into their experiences.

CHAPTER 1

What is psychometric testing?

Psychometric testing is a powerful approach to finding out about people, what makes them tick in terms of abilities, typical behaviours and motivations. The power of psychometrics can be helpful, then, to an employer, but also to you as a candidate or existing employee. However, for you to get the most out of being on the receiving end of psychometrics and produce your most brilliant performance, you need to have some understanding of the subject and you may need to build up your confidence in dealing with it. That's what this book is all about.

'Psycho' and 'metric' – how do they fit together?

The word 'psychometric' is one that many people have come across, but what it refers to is often poorly understood. Literally, it is 'psycho' - 'mental' and 'metric' – 'measurement', so psychometric testing is 'mental measurement'. It comes within the field of psychology – the study of thought, feeling and behaviour, and is one of the parts of psychology that use numbers. That is, measurement is applied to those thoughts, feelings and behaviours.

But why is mental measurement important? The answer is that it can provide better understanding of what individuals will or can do. That understanding can be useful to employers in making hiring or promotion decisions, to coaches, counsellors and the 'helping professions' generally and to people themselves as they think about career choices or personal development. In fact, psychometric testing is part of the subject of 'individual differences' – a major sub-field of psychology. (Psychologists also use numbers in studying whole groups of people and trying to make sense of consistent patterns of behaviour, for example in terms of the behaviour of crowds in riot or panic situations and how people as a whole learn language.)

Scope of psychometrics

For most people it will be the employment situation, being psychometrically tested as part of a recruitment or promotion process, that will be the main point of interest in this book and this is indeed its focus. Psychometric tests are also used in education and in clinical applications, both of which are outside the scope of this text. They have been around in one form or another for over a 100 years and early versions of some of the tests still in use today go back to the 1930s. In fact, between the late nineteenth century and the present day there were many developments in psychometrics applied to the world of work. The terms 'occupational psychology' and hence 'occupational testing' were coined in this period.

How to use this book

This first chapter sets out some basic ideas and I suggest it is at least skimmed by every reader. Practical Brilliant Tips, Brilliant Actions and Brilliant Examples appear throughout the book and these are intended to be points of focus for you as a test taker to help you in understanding what you should actually do. In Chapter 2, I explore some of the factors that might hold someone back from putting their best foot forward and how they might get over these and begin to demonstrate their brilliance. This is something to look at in detail particularly if you have had doubts about or negative experiences with psychometrics in the past. In particular I have tried to set psychometrics in the context of the overall recruitment or promotion scene. If you are concerned at the outset that you have been or might be unfairly treated through the use of psychometrics, then you should read Chapter 2 together with Chapter 8, which explore what is involved in fair testing and how to mount a challenge if you feel you need to.

Chapters 3 and 4 cover the main types of testing, ability and personality in some detail and at the end of the former there are a number of examples to work through. You will find further examples by going to the web-based material indicated in Appendix 1. For getting a real feel for what psychometrics are like, these are the chapters on which to concentrate.

Like pretty well everything else, computers are heavily used in psychometrics and if you anticipate that you will be asked to take a test delivered in this way, then you should look at Chapter 5. If your interest in the computer side of testing has a strong element of general curiosity about it, then you will also want to read Chapter 9, which deals with a range of new developments, a number of which inevitably involve the use of computer technology.

Many people will have (or will) come across those 'cousins' of psychometric tests, the structured interview, the assessment centre, the self-screener and the 360° assessment. As a candidate you are as likely to encounter the structured interview or assessment centre as psychometric tests proper, or in conjunction with them. If you know that you are going to be asked to go through these sorts of procedures then you should study Chapters 6 and 7.

Examples of psychometrics

Most psychometric tests in use today are in the form of a series of items to which candidates or participants are asked to respond, usually by choosing from alternatives. The term 'item' is usually used, rather than 'question', because not all of the material will strictly be in the form of a question, as in the

Brilliant Example below. (On another little bit of terminology, it is expected that most people using this book will be interested in doing so because they have been, or expect to be, candidates for a job. Of course someone thinking about a choice of career is not quite in the same category, nor is someone who is trying to understand why they don't fit in too well with a particular team. However, for the sake of simplicity, the term 'candidate' will be used in most cases in the text, with exceptions made only when that use would be confusing.)

 **example**

The following are some test item types:

From the alternatives given below choose the one that describes you most and the one that describes you least.

1   a. I like to relax with friends

    b. I prefer to spend my spare time alone

    c. Some people see me as reserved

    d. I like to make work fun

2   a. I resent being told what to do

    b. I like to have an outline of my duties

    c. I feel safest with very clear guidelines

    d. I can usually work out the best way of tackling a task

Choose the word from each of the alternatives given that best fits each of the following sentences.

1   Vehicles with lower carbon emissions help to . . . global warming.

    a. eliminate   b. exacerbate   c. reduce   d. marginalise

2   Cats and dogs are treasured by many people as....

    a. pets   b. children   c. guards   d. vermin

Typically such tests are in what has for a long time been known as 'paper and pencil' form, with a printed test booklet and a printed answer sheet. Nowadays this paper and pencil format is quite often transferred to the computer screen, something to which we shall return, particularly in Chapter 5.

Other formats for psychometric tests will be encountered from time to time, particularly by those going for highly specialised jobs. For example, when I was involved in selecting scientists to work in the NASA Shuttle Spacelab programme, I was conscious that they would, of course, be wearing gloves for all of their work outside the spaceship. Work inside the vessel also required considerable manual dexterity. I therefore used a specific test to assess their dexterity. It consisted of getting candidates to place as many dots as they could within a small square in a limited period of time. There are also some psychometric tests aimed at directly measuring characteristics like persistence, for example by seeing how long someone will persevere with a mechanical puzzle that doesn't actually have a solution or in reading material that is made difficult by the omission of punctuation or mixing capitals and lower case letters.

Other paper and pencil tests include tasks such as sentence completion, as in the Brilliant Example below. These are far less commonly used than the other types, partly because their interpretation is particularly complicated. There is more on these in Chapter 4.

 **example**

Here are some sentence completion examples:

● I feel miserable if ....

● My best friend ....

● Most young people ....

● If I could change anything about myself ....

....

Two other approaches to candidate assessment which use some of the ideas and principles of psychometric testing are structured interviews and assessment centres. They are included, in Chapters 6 and 7 respectively, because they will often be encountered alongside or instead of psychometric tests as such. Indeed assessment centres more often than not include one or more psychometric tests. To leave assessment centres out of consideration could be to leave you unprepared for what you are likely to face amongst the processes used in making recruitment or promotion decisions.

Definitions and illustrations

Ability and aptitude

These two terms are sometimes used rather loosely, but the ideas are distinct. 'Ability' and 'ability testing' is to do with a power to perform something, while 'aptitude' should be used for tests meant to predict a future performance, for example after a period of training. We shall mostly be concerned with ability rather than aptitude testing, though a form of aptitude testing, concerned with trainability, is covered in the last chapter.

> ability tests have been described as measures of *maximum* performance

Ability tests have been described as measures of *maximum* performance. That is, they measure how well someone can perform on some dimension of behaviour. The dot placement test mentioned above is one example, if a rather unusual one.

Measures of numerical, verbal, spatial (see Figure 1.1) and abstract reasoning (see Figure 1.2) are more common. Of these types you are particularly likely to experience numerical and verbal tests and there are quite a lot of them on the market, covering a range of difficulty levels.

Which of the shapes is not the same as the shape above?

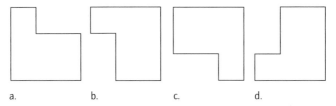

a.   b.   c.   d.

Answer: b. The rest can be rotated to fit.

Figure 1.1 Spatial reasoning example

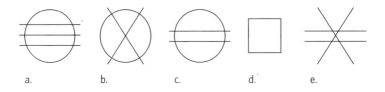

Which of the diagrams below do not fit in with the ones above? (There may be more than one.)

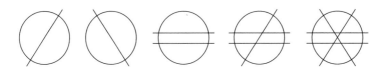

a.   b.   c.   d.   e.

Answer: a., d. and e. There is always a circle and never more than two horizontal lines.

Figure 1.2 Abstract reasoning example

Personality

Personality psychometrics is sometimes described as measuring a person's *typical* performance. That is, things like the style of interaction with others, their approach to tasks, and the level of energy they will display, which together make up the ways in which people come to be known as individuals. If there were no such typical behaviours, captured in everyday terms like outgoingness, conscientiousness and restlessness, we would have no need for the term 'personality'.

To the potential employer the attraction of using a personality measure is that it can often provide quite a detailed understanding of a candidate and do that quite quickly and efficiently. (From the employer's point of view, how much better to know in advance that a candidate is likely to be aggressive when crossed and to lack attention to detail, than to find that out after they have been appointed!) Personality measures are often referred to as questionnaires, regardless of whether or not all of their items can strictly be regarded as questions.

Sometimes personality measures will ask you to rate a statement in terms of how far you agree with it, often on a three or five point scale, as in the Brilliant Example shown below.

brilliant example

The following are examples of personality items with rating responses:

- I like to check my work in detail

    a. true   b. in between   c. false

- I don't suffer fools gladly

    a. strongly agree   b. agree

    c. neither agree nor disagree   d. disagree

    e. strongly disagree

Other personality measures force you to make choices between two or more alternatives, as in the first Brilliant Example in this chapter. One of the widely used measures using the first approach, involving rating, is the Sixteen Personality Questionnaire Version 5 (16PF5) and one using the second, forced choice, approach is Gordon's Personal Profile and Inventory (GPP-I). The Occupational Personality Questionnaire (OPQ), is available in alternative forms using both the rating and forced choice approach. Yet another widely used measure, Wave, employs both approaches in the same personality questionnaire. There is more about these different approaches and their implications for you as a test-taker in Chapter 4. For the moment, it is worth noting that you will almost certainly find it harder to make the choices *between* statements than to rate *single* statements. The person administering the test to you and/or giving you feedback on it will know that. You may feel a little better by expressing how difficult you found it to make a choice between, say, going to a tennis tournament and attending a rock concert. If you go on about that, though, you are unlikely to make any change in the interpretation of the results made and may just come across as awkward!

Ability *versus* personality

The big difference between the tests of ability and the common measures of personality are that they actually get people to produce a 'performance' as opposed to rating or choosing between descriptions of performance. This difference is highlighted by the term 'self-description inventory', which is sometimes applied to the personality measures.

Motivation

'Motivation' is sometimes seen as an elusive term and there is some debate as to whether it is really something distinct from personality. One definition of motivation in the workplace is 'the direction and the way in which people will most willingly exert effort', which arguably *does* add something to personality. However, measures of motivation are far less commonly used in recruitment than are those of personality. In a period of over 40 years working with psychometrics I have come across only three or four organisations making use of specific measures of motivation as opposed to hundreds using personality questionnaires and ability tests. Reviews and guides to testing list far fewer motivational than personality measures and not all of the leading psychometric publishers have them.

Measures of motivation are usually set out in formats similar to personality measures, with either ratings or forced choices. Again, the interesting Wave measure combines motivation and talent in a single questionnaire. As that is now quite commonly used it probably represents the most likely way in which, as a candidate, your motivation is likely to be probed. The interaction between personality and motivation is discussed again in Chapter 4.

Beware confusion

Setting aside the motivation measures for the moment, there are some people who think the term 'psychometric' applies solely to personality measures and a more or less equal number who think it applies just to measures of ability or aptitude. As should already be obvious, it applies to both and, in fact, to the measures of motivation too. It is not clear to me why this confusion exists as all the reference books, including dictionaries of psychological terms, use it correctly. As a candidate you will do well to be alert to this common confusion and try to avoid it yourself. Thus, if invited to take part in some psychometric tests with no further explanation, you might want to establish just what the hiring organisation thinks they mean by that! Also, you will appear more credible to those using the term correctly if you do.

You will not do yourself any favours in terms of credibility if you slip into another common error, that of using the term 'psychosomatic' instead of 'psychometric'. As many readers will undoubtedly know, 'psychosomatic' is an adjective used to describe diseases caused or aggravated by mental stress. (Some people may think that this is an unnecessary labouring of an obvious point, but I have been surprised at how common the error is. I came across it once in a colleague who planned to set himself up as consultant in testing. He looked rather sheepish and was not grateful when I pointed his error out to him, but I may at least have saved him from the expense of having useless business cards printed.)

How tests work

Standardisation

A key thing to note about psychometrics is that they are standardised procedures. This means that they are meant to be used in standardised ways and that applies to how they are administered and to how they are interpreted. Administration includes the use of standard instructions, which can seem a bit 'wooden' at times, but are meant to ensure that everyone taking the test has the same experience. Standard administration also includes working in a quiet and uninterrupted environment and with access to the necessary tools to do the test, including rough paper for working notes, calculators where applicable and even a visible clock in the case of a timed test. Other tools include pens or pencils and erasers for corrections. (Obvious as these conditions may seem, they are by no means always met. On the very day that I drafted this paragraph I was in conversation with a director in a local authority, who told me that during his recruitment process he had been given one propelling pencil to take a reasoning test. The lead kept breaking, interfering with his performance.) There is more about standardisation in Chapter 5 on computer-based testing and in Chapter 8 on fairness.

This standardisation of process is very different from conventional interviews in which there is often little system, questions are often worded ambiguously and some candidates are prompted. That is rather like making up the test items on the fly, and applying different ones to different people and sometimes choosing to give them the answers! Thus the standardisation of the test process is better calculated to provide everyone with the same experience, giving a basis for realistic comparison amongst the candidates and altogether contributing to decision-making that is fair.

Norm groups

As well as comparing one candidate with another, 'on the day' psychometrics provide the basis for comparison of the day's candidates with a relevant representative sample of people. This process of benchmarking is one of the key ways in which the 'metric' part of psychometrics is brought into play. Think about the case of graduate recruitment. Knowing that on, say, a verbal reasoning test, Tom scored higher than Dick or Harry might encourage the company to hire Tom. However, if comparison with a large group of graduates suggested that all three of them performed much lower than the average, that would give a better basis for decision-making and encourage the company to look further. On the other hand, if comparison with the same group showed that, despite some differences, all three were typical of the very best in the comparison group, the company might want to hire all three of them. Finding people on whom to try out the tests and so form the 'norm' groups, so that relevant comparisons can be made, is part of the process of standardising tests.

Thus the process of comparison with a standard group allows the potential employer to gain some understanding of where each candidate sits overall and of how important actual differences in scores might be. The comparison groups are known as 'norm' groups and the scores produced by these norm groups are shown in norm tables, which are used to interpret the scores produced. How the comparisons with the norm groups are made is described in the next section.

Percentiles

The remark, 'There are three kinds of lies: lies, damned lies and statistics' has been attributed, somewhat dubiously, to the Victorian Prime Minister, Benjamin Disraeli. The truth behind the remark is that it is easy to confuse and be confused by statistics. Unfortunately, psychometric testing is very much bound up with statistics. Indeed many statistical practices and terms used in other fields evolved in the pioneering days of psychometric development in the late nineteenth and early twentieth century. One of the potential sources of confusion is that there are at least three standard ways of comparing an individual test result with the performance of the norm group. However, to keep matters as simple as possible, I shall just refer here to one way: the use of percentiles. This is the most common way in which results from ability and aptitude tests are shown, but I shall touch on some other approaches briefly later in the book.

Percentile is defined as: the position of a score indicated in relation to the percentage of values in the norm group falling at or below that score. So if a candidate's score of, say, 34 items correct is higher than that achieved by 40 per cent of the norm group, it would be described as being at the 40th percentile. This is illustrated in Table 1.1. Sometimes people get confused by taking a percentile to be a percentage of the possible score. But that is to miss out the idea of the comparison group. The test shown in Table 1.1 has 50 items, so a candidate getting a score of 25 would have got 50 per cent of them right, but would have reached only the 10th percentile. As Table 1.1 indicates the actual score is often referred to as the 'raw score'. The percentile is one form of 'standardised score'.

Table 1.1 Example of raw scores and percentiles

Raw score	Percentile
0–19	1
20–22	3
23–24	5
25–27	10
28–29	15
30	20
31	25
32	32
33	35
34	40
35	45
36	50
37	60
38	70
39	75
40	80
41	85
42–43	90
44	95
45–46	97
47–50	99

It is worth making sure that you are clear on this before moving on. I have known people who have claimed to understand it, but really have not. It can be quite disheartening, if you don't understand it, to learn that you performed at the 50th percentile on a test on which you thought you had done well. You may, indeed, have got most, that is more than 50 per cent, of the items right, but if half of the norm group did too, then you will have achieved no more than the 50th percentile. Also, note that scores are not reported above the 99th or below the 1st percentile, so we don't speak in terms of parts of a percentile or refer to the hundredth percentile, even if all items are correct.

Limitations

Too much reliance?

There are some people who swear by the use of psychometric tests. Although psychometric practitioners are trained not to make exaggerated claims and, indeed, to warn candidates and clients of their limitations, some are unduly optimistic about what they can offer. As a candidate you may want to ask about how the results will be used and, particularly with measures of ability, whether a cut-off will be applied or how much weight will be put on the findings. This may not only have the result of informing you, but also raising in the mind of the test user that they need to be clear with the ultimate decision-maker as to the importance that should properly be placed on the test.

I think the days are gone when, as one leading light of testing, L.J. Cronbach claimed in 1966, 'Interpretations of test data are daily creating better lives by guiding a man into a suitable life-work...'. However, many users seem less alert to the need to educate their clientele as to the limitations of psychometrics and a little prompting here may well help. People have been wary of accepting a candidate with less than a 50th percentile score on a particular test, not recognising that a score at the 40th percentile would still represent the *average* range and show that the candidate was quite typical of a relevant comparison group.

Skills of the test user

This question of interpretation of the test to the ultimate decision-maker is one aspect of the skill of the test user. Such people will have been trained in most cases, not only in the use of the particular test that they are using, but in the initial choice of test too. That should mean that the right things are being measured and that, in the case of ability tests, the difficulty level of the test and the choice of norm group for comparative purposes is right. Such training is relatively recent, but does now seem to be widely accepted in the UK. Broadly, it is divided into 'level A' covering ability and aptitude measures and 'level B' for personality questionnaires. It is right to expect that those interpreting your test results should have the requisite training and to challenge, or at least ask, if you have any doubts.

Not in the mood?

For the most part psychometric measures deal with quite constant aspects of how someone will behave, rather than changeable states such as mood. Indeed their design will include standards of reliability, so that if you take the same test on two separate occasions you should, by and large, produce the same results. Your personality will not have changed to be the opposite of what it was over, say, a three month period and you will not suddenly have turned from a dunce at numerical reasoning into a genius. The reliability shown in a well-constructed test will reflect this. However, if you have suffered a major life-changing event such as a bereavement, you may well appear as somewhat less resilient than normal and a raging head cold or painful toothache, may well knock a few points off your performance on an ability test.

> psychometric measures will include standards of reliability

So, just as your blood pressure might fluctuate under extremes of stress, so might your test performance. Yet neither blood pressure nor the test results are likely to swing from one end of the scale to the other even under the direst stresses. There will be a fundamental 'resting level' in each case. But because your test performance will not be immune to these disturbances, you will be well advised as far as in your control to avoid taking tests under these circumstances. If events conspire against you to make this difficult or impossible, then do at least inform the test administrator who should make a note of your problem. Although it will be difficult to gauge just how much allowance will or should be made, if you do not voice the matter, none will be.

Knowledge

In general psychometric tests are not used to measure existing knowledge, but there are some exceptions. Some organisations have done this through questionnaires, an example was in the financial services industry where candidates were asked to answer questions exploring their knowledge of financial regulations. If you are a candidate for a job, say, as an insurance salesperson, you might find yourself asked to complete one of these questionnaires.

Knowledge is, of course, often explored in a conventional interview. Sometimes this approach is extended by the use of a technical interviewer, a specialist who may sit alongside a regular interviewer. Such people are quite often used when recruitment companies are involved in the hiring process.

Another exception is with regard to more junior jobs and particularly for people seeking to move into a line of work for the first time. The argument runs that if you are serious about a type of job you will have taken the trouble to find out something about it. This is assessed for instance, in the Job Knowledge Index, which poses knowledge questions about different careers.

There is also a common view that the more senior a job is, the less relevant specialist technical knowledge becomes, whereas the capacity to strategise, to understand complex new situations quickly and to provide leadership becomes ever more important. It is, of course, in the assessment of these areas that psychometric testing, as represented by ability and personality measures, comes into its own.

Doesn't my career speak for itself?

You may feel, particularly if you have been around and been successful for quite a while, that your success to date should tell the hiring organisation much of what they need to know about you. The users of psychometric tests do recognise the importance of what people have done in the past, at least in general terms. For example a 'health warning' that I put on the reports that I produce following psychometric assessment, runs as follows:

Although likely to provide some useful insights, the results of personality and ability measures, such as those reported on here, should not be used in isolation to make hiring decisions. Rather, they should be applied in conjunction with other information, such as that arising from the candidate's career history.

The problem with career history is that it rarely tells the whole story. As well as the technical content of what someone has done in the past becoming less relevant as they seek to move upwards, people often seek 'sideways moves' into areas where only part of what they have done before will have a bearing on the new job. This would be the case, for instance, of the high grade technical specialist, seeking a role where the technical expertise is to be applied in the development of policy or in giving advice to a 'political' clientele. Characteristics such as communication to non-specialists, diplomacy and influence are all likely to be important and there may be very little to go on in the previous career. In these situations it is through the value of systematic measurement that psychometrics can, again, have a useful contribution to make, helping to add objectivity and fairness to the recruitment process.

CHAPTER 2

The test mindset – how to approach psychometric testing

Motivation

Not taking it seriously

A candidate for a senior post was doing a psychometric test online in a testing suite at the offices of the potential employer. Part way through the process he managed to get the details of a test match on his screen. He did not do particularly well on the test! As well as suggesting something a bit odd about the administrative arrangements that enabled him to access sport, it was also taken as indicative of his lack of motivation for the process.

brilliant tip

Give it your best shot and you are most likely to produce your best result.

Do I have to do this at all?

Out of the tens of thousands of people I have seen through psychometric assessment, I have known only a handful who have flatly refused to take a psychometric test or tests. Rather more have questioned why they are being asked to go through the requested process and a few have indicated disquiet about a specific test.

Perhaps not surprisingly, if you absolutely refuse to go through the psychometrics requested, you will create a poor impression on those involved in the recruitment process. To begin with you raise the problem of what to do with the lack of psychometric evidence from you and the wealth of it that they have from the other candidates. So, do they abandon that information, along with all the time and expense that they have taken to get it, or do they proceed with less information about you, which could affect you positively or negatively? If other candidates learn that you have not gone through the same procedure as them and, particularly if you are the one who gets appointed, they may well make a formal complaint, giving the hiring organisation another headache. Rather than go to that trouble the recruiters are more likely to take the line that you cannot really be serious about wanting the job and cut you adrift without more ado. This is another way in which an apparent lack of motivation about testing can damage your chances.

brilliant tip

Be careful about how you question the psychometric process and don't just refuse to take it.

How motivated am I?

If you are having doubts about how motivated you are to do the psychometric testing, then it may be worth considering if it is really the testing that is the problem or if that is actually just an excuse and there is really something else that you don't like about the job concerned. If it is the psychometrics, then it will be worthwhile continuing with this chapter and the rest of the book, which should help you to become more comfortable with the whole psychometric experience. If it is really the job itself, then that, of course, is something for you to think about separately.

You might feel that taking a test and having a record kept of your performance on it is something of an invasion of privacy. However, consider how useful it is for a potential employer – and actually for you – to have assessed relevant aspects of your makeup and to have that on record for purposes of reference (see also chapter 8 on testing fairly).

How can I improve or can I improve at all?

Personality *versus* ability

As noted in Chapter 1, there is a difference between personality and ability psychometrics captured in the terms 'typical' and 'maximum performance'. This distinction is important as you think about how you might do differently on a test. In terms of ability, setting aside the question of changes in ability as such, covered at the end of this chapter, it is really a question of putting your best foot forward. In other words, thinking about how you can make sure that the maximum ability that you demonstrate in the test is actually the maximum of which you are capable. To go beyond that, would, of course be to present a picture of yourself that exaggerates your actual ability. In a few cases people have done that when making internal applications by the expedient of stealing tests and marking keys from colleagues' desks, actually breaking into them. In one incident this was not definitely proven, but the improvement in the candidate's performance from a previous test occasion was so marked that the new results were just set aside by the company concerned.

> it is really a question of putting your best foot forward

Others have not gone quite as far as breaking and entering, but have used trickery to lay their hands on the tests that they would be taking and sought to gain advantage in that way. In one such situation the trust of a team member was abused by a former colleague, who claimed to be considering the use of a particular ability measure and wanted to know more about it. The staff member showed him the details of the test concerned and let him 'have a go' at it. He learnt that his former colleague knew that he was going to experience the test himself a few days later, that he did quite well at it and was subsequently appointed to the job. The story does have a moral: the culprit only lasted a couple of months in the new position!

So, what is discussed here is not about falsifying an ability test result, but about getting the most accurate result for you.

Right and wrong answers

Personality psychometrics are sometimes introduced with the statement, 'there are no right or wrong answers' and this is often followed by the suggestion that you should not dwell for too long on any one item, but respond as spontaneously as possible. All of this is to encourage you to give as true a representation of yourself as possible by being honest in your responses. However, I find the claim about right and wrong answers somewhat dishonest, or at least naive. I also feel that the view (quite often strongly expressed by those using personality measures) that they are not tests, lacking in candour. When a personality measure is used it is because the hiring organisation – or those working on its behalf – has a view of the patterns of personality that will suit them in the job. Thus they may have sales profiles, general management profiles and profiles for project managers. It is against these that the candidate is being assessed through the personality questionnaire. Therefore it is being used as a test.

So, what does this mean for you as a candidate? First of all, don't be lulled into a false sense of security. The personality questionnaire is there for a reason and although organisations vary tremendously in the store that they will set by it, few will

put aside the results completely and most will be uncomfortable with a candidate who presents a profile that is greatly
different from what has been specified.

So what should your approach be in the case of personality questionnaires? If you want to present a picture of yourself that is
more in line with the requirements of the job than you believe
yourself to be, you may have some success in doing so. There was
a study, for instance, indicating
that when asked to answer the
Gordon Personal Profile and
Inventory as if they were salespeople, those taking part in a
laboratory study were able to
produce a fair representation of

> don't be lulled into a false
> sense of security. The
> personality questionnaire
> is there for a reason

a salesperson's profile. There are, however, pitfalls in doing that
and, as will be seen in more detail in Chapter 4, these include
showing up on a variety of 'impression management scales' and
getting caught out during feedback. Also, to portray a false
impression 'usefully' in the sense of increasing your chances of
getting a job you will need to have a good idea of your own real
characteristics, how these are likely to differ from the required
job profile and how the profile characteristics are captured in the
questionnaire you are undertaking. Notwithstanding the study
result above, this can be quite a tall order!

Then there is the question of why you should want to portray a
false picture of your personality? The answer may be that you
are desperate for a job and don't think that your actual personality profile will fit you for it. That again rather assumes that
you have good understanding of yourself and of the job in order
to make that judgement. But let's take the case of a job requiring attention to detail, such as a health and safety inspector
perhaps. If you do not possess that characteristic, but manage
to project the impression that you do, if hired you will probably
find the work highly uncongenial and will be unlikely to last

long in it. So again it should really be a matter of putting your best foot forward in the short term and possibly making some further investment of time and effort to make certain changes in the longer term, as discussed below.

 **tip**

Don't try to second guess what the questions in a personality measure are trying to get at.

Things you can do, short term

If the reason for a lack of performance is to do with lack of confidence about taking psychometric tests or lack of familiarity with the testing environment or lack of understanding as to what is required, then you almost certainly can improve. Let's look at these issues and at some other common barriers.

Lack of confidence

Some people think that the testing situation will be like the exams they experienced at school, which are a source of discomfort for many. Of course the format of exams differs from subject to subject, but in many subjects there is still some emphasis on learning by rote. There are some tests that do assess knowledge and these come under the further heading of 'attainment' tests. They are applied in educational rather than employment settings. The psychometrics that you will experience as a candidate don't assess your knowledge of German irregular verbs or the cash crops harvested in sub-Saharan Africa. Thus the knowledge component is minimal or non-existent, with the focus of the ability tests on the reasoning that you can apply and that of the personality questionnaires on your characteristic – typical – ways of behaving. (If you are not convinced of that now, you may be after progressing to Chapters 3 and 4 or after exploring some of the tests reached by the various links indicated at the end of the book.) Some of the few exceptions where knowledge is subject to a form of test were discussed in Chapter 1 and they really are exceptions!

You may be underconfident about taking a test because you have some form of disability, such as dyslexia. There are ways to handle the problems that can arise from such conditions and knowing that is the case should help you feel more comfortable with the psychometric tests that you are to experience. Those responsible for setting up the test

those responsible should ask you if you have any special requirements

procedures should ask you if you have any special requirements. Whether they actually do so or not, it is important that you do let them know about the problems that you may experience. In many cases they will be able to make special arrangements, such as providing large print copies of test booklets for those with impaired vision. However this all needs to be planned in advance. This subject is returned to in Chapter 8, on testing fairly.

Previous experience of poor test performance can be a real barrier for some people. Of course it may be that there is a serious lack of ability, but that is not always the case as the Brilliant Example illustrates. Coaching with sample material as used there is one way to get over this problem.

brilliant example

Increasing familiarity to optimise brilliance

Joe Jones was a senior director in a local authority. Seeking a change of career, he applied for a high level job in the civil service, but was horrified to learn that he would be expected to take a test of numerical reasoning

▶

ability. He anticipated, rightly, that this would be quite a tough one and he reflected uncomfortably on the fact that he had performed very poorly on such a test a few years before. Although not regarding himself as very strong in this area, he felt that he had always managed to get by and the thought of missing out again because of the hurdle that the test represented became quite upsetting to him. He had never understood his poor performance on the previous occasion and had just hoped that he would never be confronted with such a test again.

The approach adopted for helping him was to take him first through some sample numerical test material and to look in detail at how he approached and coped with that. No major problems arose, although he was helped to see where he was making a couple of mistakes fairly systematically. Without taking him progressively through more and more difficult sample material (one option considered) he went on to do the real test as a candidate. He did not do outstandingly, but well enough. Today he successfully heads an important government agency . . . and is no longer afraid of numerical reasoning tests.

Lack of familiarity

Lack of familiarity with tests in general or with a particular style of test can also pose a barrier to success. Although the majority of people who go through psychometric procedures have gone through one or more tests in the past, a sizeable minority have not. There are, though, many ways of becoming familiar with the process. This book is intended, among other things, to provide such familiarity and there are other sources of information, much of it made available by the leading test publishers (details of some of these sources are given in Appendix 1).

Very often the organisation that is asking you to take one or more tests will supply you with information about them, including some sample material for practice. This information may include hints and tips on the approach that you should take.

Of course you may feel that none of that pre-exposure is quite the same as experiencing the test environment itself. Typically, though, you will not just be pitchforked into responding to a series of difficult questions. The test administrator will have a set of instructions to give you and there will often be practice items for the ability tests.

'I haven't applied for a job in years' is a comment heard from candidates more often than one would expect in these days of 'no careers for life' and job changes every two or three years. It is a cry more commonly heard from those in the public than the private sector and it may really be directed at the recruitment process as a whole and a discomfort with the unfamiliarity of the whole experience. In such cases the psychometric test may just be a convenient point of focus for anxiety, though perhaps the formal presentation runs that a close second. If you are in that situation, by all means proceed with the material presented in this book, so as to renew any acquaintance that you might once have had with psychometrics. However, it may also be worth your while to refamiliarise yourself with other aspects of the recruitment process and prepare for those. (A number of other books in the *Brilliant series* will be helpful here, including *Brilliant Interview* by Ros Jay and *Brilliant CV* by Jim Bright and Joanne Earl.)

Computers and confidence

There are wide variations in the extent to which people feel at ease with the use of computers in general and we are certainly not at the stage when familiarity and comfort can be universally assumed. Different devices will be set up in different ways and so if you are asked to attend a testing session at an organisation's offices, as opposed to being sent a link to complete a test remotely, then you may find that it is not obvious how to get started. However, you can expect to be given comprehensive instructions for dealing with that aspect of the situation as well as on the test itself.

There is more on computerised testing in Chapter 5.

Strangeness of format

Some people find that the unfamiliarity of the format of test items makes them feel uncomfortable. This may apply particularly to abstract items, where the task set is necessarily far removed from everyday tasks. It can also apply to other forms as well. I was a little surprised a few years ago when using a high-level numerical reasoning test for development purposes with a group of senior engineering managers. Several of them complained that they had found the items difficult because it was obviously 'a test for accountants'. In fact there were no accountancy items as such, the test had not been constructed with accountants in mind and there were no norms for them. Some of the items did, indeed, ask people to identify things like the most profitable departments in a retail environment. However the numerical operations involved were, in fact, quite elementary compared with the calculations that the managers did routinely in running their factories and so it appeared to be the context in which they were set that led to the anxiety.

If you are worried by the idea of facing an unfamiliar format, try to remember the following Brilliant Tips.

brilliant tips

- There will be no reason to ask you to take a test designed to assess skills unrelated to the job for which you are applying. So if you want to be an advertising copywriter you will be most unlikely to be asked to take a test of mechanical comprehension.
- You will often be given sample materials in advance of the testing session and the administration of the test will as often as not include practice items.
- Books like this and other sources are readily available to give you the opportunity to familiarise yourself with items of many types.

Lack of understanding

Instructions

Yet another source of problems and also likely to result in a lack of confidence on the part of the test taker stems from a failure to understand what is required in the testing situation. This can, in turn, lead to poor performance and may colour future perceptions of and feelings towards tests in general.

Test administrators will have typically been trained in what they are doing, including presenting you with standard instruction for the tests, or getting you to read those instructions from a test booklet. Yet it is a matter of some concern that those instructions may not themselves always be clear. For example, the standard instructions for a previous version of the 16PF – a much-used personality measure that was referred to briefly in Chapter 1 – state that on most items there are no right or wrong answers. However, the last part of it comprised a number of reasoning items, which clearly do have right and wrong answers. Although there were separate instructions in the test booklet introducing that part, some candidates did not complete those items, because they thought that they were not required to do so, given the initial instruction.

The instructions for more than one reasoning test tell people to work as quickly and as accurately as possible or, as a variation on that, 'work fast, but not so fast that you make mistakes'. It does not make sense to optimise both speed and accuracy, and how are you to know how fast you can work without making mistakes? Such instructions are, frankly, nonsensical and the test publishers have never shown much interest in amending them, in effect falling back on the notion that as the tests as a whole 'work' the instructions must somehow be good enough.

All of that will be little comfort to you, the test taker, so what can you do about it? There is little point in asking the test administrator for clarification here as they will be unlikely to have a story to tell that stands outside the publisher's words. However, it may be worthwhile raising the issue in any case. If the administrator is adhering to good practice then they will keep a test log on which, among other things, any issues arising from the testing session can be raised. Certainly the fact that a candidate has reasonably pointed out that the instructions do not make sense would need to be set down and, hopefully, noted by the test user in interpreting the findings. That will not necessarily move you from the bottom to the top of the class, so to speak, but might be taken into account in marginal cases. (Also, you might be doing a service to future test users, by increasing the chance of their being asked to do tests with clearer instructions.)

That may still seem of only limited help to you, so what else can you do? See the Brilliant Tip below.

brilliant tip

First of all think about the timing in relation to the number of items. For example if the test lasts 30 minutes and there are 45 items, then you have 40 seconds to do each one. But, in fact to get a high score you won't necessarily need to get everything right. A quick examination of a number of commonly used ability tests shows that the 99th percentile is always reached with fewer than all items being answered correctly. The numbers vary from test to test of course, but you will nearly always have a margin of at least three items incorrect or incomplete to reach that level. Although that doesn't tell you exactly how to pace yourself in the tests, it does mean that you may be able to relax from a very fast pace, which could lead to unnecessary errors.

Penalties for errors?

There are some ability tests where the scoring includes penalties for errors. That is, you are not just judged on the number of items that you get right, but your score is adjusted for the number that you get wrong. In those circumstances it is obviously better not to put down an answer about which you are very doubtful and certainly to make random responses would be ill-advised. In fact the majority of ability tests do not include error penalties in their scoring and many of those that do will indicate that in the instructions, either directly or indirectly e.g. 'avoid wild guessing'.

If the instructions do not state that there is penalty scoring, you may not get any further if you seek clarification from the test administrator, who will probably be encouraged to stonewall such questions. Regardless of whether or not you are told that you will be penalised for errors, you are still likely to be better off avoiding guesswork. That is because if you just make guesses towards the end of a test when you feel that you are running out of time, you will be more likely to show more errors there, so your guessing strategy will be quite apparent when the results are examined. This could throw doubt on how seriously you took the exercise.

> you are still likely to be better off avoiding guesswork

Not reading instructions properly

From observing people taking ability tests it is quite often evident to me that the instructions have not been read properly. For example, candidates will often assume that in a multiple choice test, say of numerical reasoning, one of a number of numerical answers provided must be correct and they miss an alternative category of 'none of the above'. Similarly, with some verbal reasoning tests two answers may be correct and both of these would need to be identified for you to gain credit on that item. These points are illustrated in the following Brilliant Example.

tip

Do read the instructions carefully.

example

Based on the following passage, which of the statements below follows logically? Tick all that apply.

The use of low-energy light bulbs is just one of a number of examples of adjustments that all households can make to saving fuel and helping to slow down the effects of global warming. Take up of this simple approach has been gradual, but is now accelerating.

1   There are other ways of reducing global warming than using low energy light bulbs.

2   Most people are now using low-energy light bulbs.

3   Some people don't care about global warming.

4   The contribution of low-energy light bulbs to saving fuel is greater than it was.

Both 1 and 4 should be ticked.

Please tick the correct answer to the following from the alternatives given below.

The Blankshire Building Society saw its profits fall by 20 percent to £200 million for the half year just gone, compared to its performance in the same period last year.

Profits for the previous half year were:

a. £180 million   b. £250 million   c. £220 million   d. can't say

The correct answer is d. can't say.

Very often these variations on the usual multiple choice format of a single correct answer provided will be covered in advance sample material or in practice items at the beginning of the test. However, when there is a series of sub-tests that may not always be so. Therefore, it is important to be clear about the instructions, whether these are read to you or you are invited to read them yourself. This is a good idea even if you are given practice items, as getting something wrong at the practice stage because of not following the instructions properly could in itself be distracting and unsettling.

Not understanding the information displayed

In a recent case a candidate had been taking a reasoning test on a computer and had produced a low score, which was not in keeping with the other information about him, which had suggested better than average reasoning ability. Examination of the test record showed that he had taken only 19 minutes of the 50 allowed for the test. During a feedback session it became apparent that he had misread a thermometer-like display indicating the number of items completed for an indication of the amount of time remaining. There was a separate display indicating the latter. Thus he had rushed through the test and made lots of mistakes. One might question how someone could mistake 19 minutes for 50, but that appears to be what he did. This is the only case I know of that particular mistake arising with that particular test, but I have now taken steps to warn candidates in advance of the possibility of doing the same. Other tests will no doubt have other ways for mistakes to arise in ways that the test publishers have not anticipated. There is no substitute for following the instructions.

Not asking questions

With both ability and personality measures when administered face-to-face there is almost invariably the opportunity to ask questions if you do not understand something. The final invitation to do so is often worded along the lines of 'Are there any last questions before we begin?' I used to be surprised by the fact that that invitation was often accompanied by head-shaking, only to be followed as I raised my stopwatch and started to form the word 'begin' by interventions such as 'Just one thing' or 'So how long have I got?' This often sounds to me like reluctance to ask about something that the candidate feels probably has been covered already and so the question may make them look foolish or inattentive. I sometimes wonder about those who fail to ask their question at all and so blunder on in ignorance.

Sometimes people finally get round to asking that last burning question when the test is actually under way. If the administrator is following the instructions you may be met with a polite refusal to answer. If they take pity on the candidate the answer may be given, but at the very least some time will have been wasted. Of course it can be daunting to ask a question, whether you are taking tests as part of the 'milk round' in an examination hall with 50 other candidates, or are in a smaller room with five people who seem to understand perfectly well what they are to do, or you are a middle-aged executive and the test administrator seems young enough to be your grandchild.

brilliant tip

If you don't ask, you won't know, and you may perform below your best as a result.

Things you can do, longer term

The first thing to ask yourself in thinking about improving your performance beyond the superficial level represented by the points made above is: Do you really want to change (it might take a lot of effort)?

If there were no possibility of changing any aspects of our behaviour then there would be no work for the coaches, trainers and a host of management development specialists. But change takes a lot of effort and may not suit you. To help you think about change, consider the tips on the types of things you could try, as shown in Brilliant Tips below.

brilliant tips

- Begin by considering how you learn best. There are some tools to help you with this, such as Honey and Mumford's Learning Styles Inventory.

- Are there opportunities to practise the things that you want to improve in a non-critical environment e.g. through a hobby or by taking on responsibilities in a club or society?

- Consider if there are certain aspects of the area where you are not strong that present you with particular difficulties. For example, if you don't do well with numerical reasoning is it because you have always struggled with percentages? If so, get someone to help you in that area in particular.

- If you want to change an aspect of your typical behaviour, such as a failure to listen to others, find someone who does that well and study the detail of their behaviour.

- As you work on any change, set distinct objectives and then review how you are doing against them. Get feedback from others.

- Get yourself a coach to work with you.

None of the efforts in Brilliant Tips and others like them are likely to bring about major transformations and the rather depressing proverb, 'You can't make a silk purse out of a sow's ear', probably holds true. What you may be able to achieve, though, are the following:

- make a small amount of genuine change in the characteristic concerned;
- reflect that change in the results that you produce on one or more psychometric tests;
- find ways of managing around an area of relative deficit.

CHAPTER 3

Ability tests – what to expect

Speed and power – not a sports car, but two alternatives in testing

Most tests of ability and aptitude are designed and normed to be completed in a set time. These are speed tests and the time available will be indicated to you as a candidate at the outset. Others are tests of power and are designed to see how far you can go in handling reasoning ability. Both fit in with the description 'tests of maximum performance', but in one case it is maximum performance against the clock and in the other a sort of overall maximum. But the distinction is not complete and there are a few tests with timed and untimed norms, so they work as tests of speed *and* power.

Quite why there is so much emphasis on speed over power is not entirely clear. It is, of course, administratively convenient to have tests that run to the same time, but testing is not for the convenience of administrators and personality questionnaires are almost invariably designed to be completed without a time limit. The answer probably lies in the idea that in many aspects of work one needs to reason quickly in order to get through day-to-day tasks, but that argument is not so compelling as to suggest that a test of power might not also add value. There will be some work tasks that are very complicated and so knowing that someone has the ability to handle high levels of complexity, even if not very quickly can be very useful.

In one commonly used test where there have been attempts to combine the speed and power principles, candidates are told to work to a time limit and when that time is up they are asked to mark their answer sheet to show where they have reached. They are then given unlimited time to progress as far as they can. The idea is that this gives two scores, which can then be compared against the two sets of norms – timed for speed and untimed for power. The problem is that as the first part of the test is timed, the responses given are not being made under the conditions of a power test, where people might have lingered over some of those earlier items and perhaps improved their scores. However, the performance on the whole test is compared with the power norms. So, at best, the result is a measure of speed and a rather doubtful measure of power.

For the most part you will be unlikely to come across tests of power unless you are applying for a position where strategic thinking is a major point of emphasis. There is more about this in the last chapter, but for now the emphasis will be on tests of speed rather than power.

Numerical reasoning

Numerical tests look at the practical use of numbers and are not designed to find budding Einsteins nor even, as indicated in the last chapter, (very often) budding accountants. The operations you will be asked to perform in a numerical reasoning test will almost invariably be those of arithmetic, rather than branches of mathematics such as algebra or geometry. Pretty well all of them will give you possible answers in multiple choice format. Even for relatively simple tests you will be given rough paper on which to work. (Do make sure that you use the rough paper rather than writing on the test booklet. This is something which applies to

> the operations in a numerical reasoning test will be those of arithmetic

most tests, with the test booklets intended to be reusable. The administration instructions will nearly always mention this and you may find it embarrassing to realise that you have just incurred unnecessary cost to a potential employer by spoiling their test materials!)

For more difficult tests you will usually be provided with a calculator. Most of us are familiar with these devices, but it is worth taking a moment before you start the test to make sure that you do know how to switch on and use the one provided to you. It is as well to do this even before starting any practice items so as not to be distracted from them and what they are intended to illustrate. If no other opportunity is given to you by the test administrator to 'play' with the calculator, then take the one provided when you are asked if you have any questions. If you are anxious about using an unfamiliar calculator, then take along your own. Do ask permission to use it, which will usually be given, but don't try to do so if the test instructions say calculators are not to be used. (This may seem an obvious point, but I have known people attempting to break the rules in this way, usually I think through inattention to the instructions rather than as a result of a real attempt to cheat.)

brilliant tip

Don't let a calculator trip you up: if you are allowed to use one it is meant to be a help, not a hindrance.

If the test is to be completed in pencil and paper format you will be given an answer sheet. This will have a series of response boxes against the number of the question. In principle this should be easy enough to use, but people do sometimes manage to get out of sequence. There are usually clear instructions for what to do if you make a mistake, typically either cross or rub it out and put in your proper answer. However, getting out of sequence can be distracting and take time to correct, the more so if you only realise your mistake several items further on.

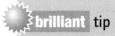 **tip**

Keep your responses in step with the questions.

Of the types of item you will be asked to deal with, some will just involve the basic arithmetical operations of addition, subtraction and multiplication, as shown in the following Brilliant Example. These will vary in difficulty from test to test.

brilliant example

Basic numerical reasoning items

Select the correct answer to the following from the alternatives given.

1 $\frac{2}{3} - \frac{1}{4}$

   a. $\frac{1}{12}$ **b.** $\frac{5}{12}$ **c.** $\frac{1}{4}$ **d.** $\frac{3}{8}$

2 49 + 16

   a. 33   **b.** 65   **c.** 75   **d.** 63

3 $\frac{14}{5}$

   a. 2.8   **b.** 70   **c.** 2.9   **d.** 3.8

4 4 × 46

   a. 148   **b.** 192   **c.** 216   **d.** 184

Other items will require the application of these basic operations in tasks such as identifying the next or missing number in a series, or involve the calculation of percentages. These are illustrated in the Brilliant Examples below, together with the correct answer and also the rationale or calculation necessary to get there.

 **example**

Applying the basic operations

A Indicate the correct number to complete each of the series below from the alternatives given.

1 6 23 40 ? 74

    a. 58   b. 46   c. 57   d. 69

    Answer is c. 57: 17 is added each time

2 39 45 43 49 47 ? 51

    a. 45   b. 6   c. 48

    Answer: a. 45: 6 is added then 2 subtracted

B Indicate the correct answers from the alternatives given.

1 Subtract 3% from 120

    a. 111.7   b. 117   c. 116.4   d. 114.6

    Answer: c. 116.4: $120 - (\frac{3}{100} \times 120) = 120 - 3.6 = 116.4$

2 What percentage of 256 is 32?

    a. 8   b. 12.5   c. 64.8   d. 16.5

    Answer: b. 12.5: $\frac{32}{256} \times 100 = .125 \times 100 = 12.5$

At middle and higher levels, the items take the form of 'problems', with a focus on interpretation of the information given as well as calculation. Part of the ability tested with such items is on making sense of the particular form of display used. These include pie charts, bar charts (the technical name is histograms), graphs and tables. These are illustrated in Figure 3.1.

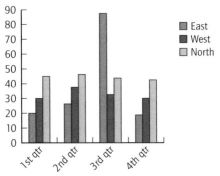

a. Histogram: Performance of regions by quarter

Disease	Clinic A	Clinic B	Clinic C
MRSA	23	12	5
C. Difficile	1	0	6

b. Table: Incidence of internal infection

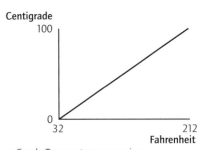

c. Graph: Temperature conversion

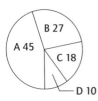

d. Pie chart: exports by percent

Figure 3.1 Displays in numerical reasoning tests

Such displays are presented alongside text setting out the problem. This text may relate to a single display as in Figure 3.2 or to two or more, as in Figure 3.3 In some cases you will be given a data card of information to be drawn on in answering the various items. Quite often there is a common story-line behind all the items, thus they may all be set in 'Joe Bloggs Engineering' or 'Acme Retail'. It is, perhaps, this element of the story-line

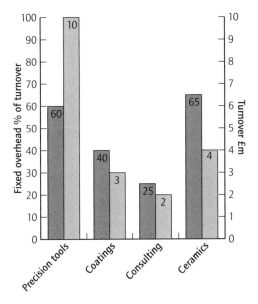

ABC manufacturing is considering the amalgamation amongst its divisions in order to save costs. It has estimated that a saving of 15 percent of its fixed overhead for each of the divisions involved could be achieved by the amalgamation of any two of them.

Please answer the following:

1. What would be the saving if Coatings is merged with Precision Tools?

a. £1.8m   b. £1.08m   c. £1.2m   d. £9m   Answer: b. £1.08m

2. What is the gross profit of Ceramics Division?

a. £4m   b. £2.6m   c. £1.5m   d. £1.4m   Answer: d. £1.4m

Figure 3.2 Numerical reasoning, one display

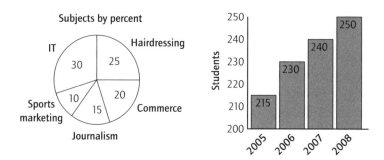

The North Greenshire College of Further Education had enrollled an increasing number of students over the last four years, but the proportion taking each subject has remained the same. Twice as many girls as boys take hairdressing, but otherwise the numbers are quite evenly matched between the genders.

1. How many students took commerce in 2005?

a. 43   b. 20   c. 5   d. 55   Answer: a. 43

2. How any students have taken IT over the last four years?

a. 220   b. 280   c. 297   d. 75   Answer: b. 280

3. How many boys enrolled in hairdressing in 2007?

a. 50   b. 20   c. 48   d. can't say   Answer: b. 20

Figure 3.3 Numerical reasoning with multiple displays

that makes some people uncomfortable with these types of items declaring, openly or to themselves for instance, 'I don't know anything about retail.' But the story-line is only there to provide a setting for the problem and there is no question of the test endeavouring to tap into engineering or retail knowledge, or whatever it may be.

The addition of text means of course that there is an element of verbal understanding necessary to respond appropriately to the item. However, this can generally be regarded as elementary compared with that required in verbal reasoning tests, which are discussed in the next section.

Other problem items do not use displays as such, but simply involve text and figures, as shown in the Brilliant Example below.

 **example**

Numerical reasoning items with text and figures

1   If population growth in Ruritania is expected to be at 186,000 per annum and the population currently stands at 6.2 million, by what percentage will it have grown over a four year period?

   a. 9.5%   **b.** 1.2%   **c.** 12%   **d.** 3%

Answer: c. 12%

There are various ways in which the different types of numerical items can be combined, but usually the problem type is separated from those which just involve calculations. Some examples of numerical reasoning tests are given at the end of this chapter.

brilliant tip

In working with the practice material in this book or from other sources treat the task seriously, giving yourself enough time and space to work undisturbed. Otherwise you might end up as confused or anxious as before you started.

It is more often with numerical reasoning tests than with other types that I have observed the 'rabbit in the headlamps' syndrome – people who seem to be transfixed with fear. They often wear their discomfort on their sleeve, announcing their anxiety as they go into the testing session. If that describes you, do look again at the Brilliant Tips in Chapter 2, as well as practising the tests at the end of the chapter and in the various links listed in Appendix 1.

Verbal reasoning

In verbal reasoning tests the aim is to measure the ability to work with the written word. There are, as with numerical reasoning, two broad categories representing two broad levels of difficulty. At the first level items include the identification of the best word to fit a gap, as in the example given in the first Brilliant Example in Chapter 1; the understanding of similar words (synonyms) and the understanding of words opposite in meaning to those given (antonyms). Examples of each of these types of item are given in the following Brilliant Example.

 **example**

Simple verbal reasoning items

A Synonyms

For each item choose the word from the alternatives given that is most similar in meaning.

1 Pledge

a. promise   b. curse   c. request   d. bill

Answer: a. promise

2 Dandy

    a. bully   **b.** fop   **c.** courtier   **d.** dancer

    Answer: b. fop

B Antonyms

For each item choose the word from the alternatives given that is most nearly opposite in meaning.

1 Insubordinate

    a. obedient   **b.** unruly   **c.** outdoors   **d.** careless

    Answer: b. unruly

2 Disputatious

    a. argumentative   **b.** accommodating

    c. litigious   **d.** poorly

    Answer: a. argumentative

brilliant tip

Obviously, you need to know the words in question to be able to perform well on such tasks. However, even if you don't know the specific word that is the right answer you might manage to perform satisfactorily if you know the other words. For example in A2 in the Brilliant Example, you might not know the word 'fop', but if you do know the meanings of 'bully', 'courtier' and 'dancer' you will be aware that they do not fit, so it becomes obvious that 'fop' is the correct answer. In B2 you might not know the word 'disputatious', but see that it is to do with 'dispute', which might be a word that you do know.

However you go about reaching the right answer, either by knowledge or by working it out, you can see that good performance is dependent on having a good vocabulary, sometimes referred to as your 'word power'. There are some other things involved here, too. As these tests are timed – tests of speed – if you are a slow reader you are unlikely to do well. There is also a need to be able to make sense of the phrase or sentence in which a missing word sits. This can be demanding in the case of items with double negatives or those involving quite long sentences, as in the Brilliant Example below.

 **example**

Simple in principle but more complicated in practice

A   **Missing word(s) in sentence with double negative.**

John was not disinclined to go to the party, as he expected that some of his .... would be there.

a. enemies   b. mates

c. boring relatives   d   most disliked colleagues

B   **Missing word in long sentence.**

There are few if any excuses available to a manager whose team keeps losing and, as recent history keeps telling us with its parade of departed managers, little patience on the part of the boards of clubs with such .... no matter how popular a character is involved, what range of injuries have been sustained by the players or how strong the competition.

a. successes   b. matches   c. failures   c. leagues

brilliant tip

So how can you do your best with these tests? As with numerical reasoning, do pay attention to your timing. Also, read the items carefully, so as not to get tripped up by, say, a double negative. Another tip here, though it does take time, is to make a note of the double negative element and cross the two negatives out. So in A. above, crossing out 'not' and 'dis', leaves you with, 'John was inclined to go to the party', which should help you to see that 'mates' is the right answer. You will not be as quick with that approach as you will be if you can actually take double negatives in your stride, but you will have a way of tackling such items.

Test of 'pure' vocabulary are used either alone or as part of composite tests. The argument for their use is that word power is itself a predictor of performance in some jobs. However, as such tests are nearly always timed, reading speed again comes into play.

In the second type of verbal reasoning test the tasks are more complicated. They involve passages of prose and then several items relating to each of them. The items require the candidate to interpret the information in the passages, but the specific tasks vary from test to test and often within the test. Thus, to do well you need to be able to understand the information in the passage and also to understand exactly what the task is. That may range from very strict deduction to identifying what might be true – might be inferred – but does not follow absolutely logically. Two examples are given in the Brilliant Example overleaf and you will come across more in the practice tests at the end of the chapter.

> word power is itself a predictor of performance in some jobs

⊙▶ brilliant example

Verbal reasoning: deduction

Tim and Mary were discussing some of their friends. Tim knew that Charles was older than Jean, but didn't know if Jason was younger than her or not. Mary didn't know Charles, but did know his twin brother, Steve, whom she knew to be younger than Jason.

What can be deduced from the passage above?

1   Tim and Mary have a lot of friends between them.

    a. true   **b.** false   **c.** can't say

    Answer: c. can't say. We are told that they are discussing some of their friends; only four are mentioned and we don't know if there are many more or just a few.

2   Jason is older than Jean.

    a. true   **b.** false   **c.** can't say

    Answer: a. true. Jason is older than Charles who we know is older than Jean.

3   Charles is much older than Steve.

    a. true   **b.** false   **c.** can't say

    Answer: b. false. Charles and Steve are twins so must be very close in age.

 **example**

Verbal reasoning: inference

Many people are becoming conscious of environmental issues and trying to change their own habits. The buying of smaller cars is one trend and another is an increased tendency to reuse plastic bags. Yet some people are questioning if their efforts will be far outweighed by the development of more coal-fired power stations and the waste represented by lighting office buildings out of working hours.

Which of the following can be inferred from the above passage?

1   If people could put more environmentally-friendly fuel into their cars at no extra cost they would be likely to do so.

    a. true   **b.** false   **c.** can't say

    Answer: a. true. This would fit in with the other changes in habits indicated.

2   Initiatives to supply the energy gap by burning more fossil fuels will be unhesitatingly welcomed.

    a. true   **b.** false   **c.** can't say

    Answer: b. false. If people are questioning coal-fired power stations they are unlikely to welcome the use of fossil fuels of any type.

3   Domestic sales of solid fuel are likely to decline.

    a. true   **b.** false   **c.** can't say

    Answer: c. can't say. It is not clear if people know how domestic solid fuel compares with electricity, gas or oil in its environmental impact and so how favourably or not they would regard it.

There are a couple of things worth thinking about in preparation for these higher level verbal reasoning tests. The first is to set aside any information that you may have about the situation depicted in the passage and treat what is presented as fact. For most people this is not usually much of a problem as the topics chosen are often a little out of the way whilst still being comprehensible to the ordinary person. So, if there were an item on, say, poisonous snakes and you had made a special study of that subject your special knowledge could intrude. Poisonous snakes might well be taken as a topic; everyone knows what they are, but few of us have studied them in depth.

 **tip**

> With the complex verbal reasoning tests, set aside any existing knowledge.

The advice 'read (and/or listen to) the instructions' applies with particular force to the higher level verbal reasoning tests. This is because the task set, being verbal, has to be set up through words to a greater extent than many of the other types of test. Candidates who score poorly on a particular sub-test have sometimes clearly got onto the wrong wavelength, for example treating an inference item as one of deduction.

brilliant tip

> Pay particular attention to the instructions for verbal reasoning tests.

Abstract reasoning

You are less likely to come across tests of abstract reasoning than those of numerical or verbal ability, though they are sometimes employed at very senior levels. The reasoning for doing so is that they give information on a candidate's ability to cope with complexity in forms that are new to them and high scorers will have a good chance of working effectively in high level roles in an organisation where what is going on is largely new to them. Another part of the reasoning is that such tests also measure strategic thinking.

The form of these tests usually involves a series of arrangements of drawings. You are asked to identify which of a number of alternatives agree with a sample set, as shown in the example in Figure 1.2, choose the next arrangement or pick a missing one. The arrangements do not represent anything in the real world, nor are you required to consider the manipulation of figures as in the mechanical and spatial tests described below.

brilliant tips

- A number of different rules may apply to any one series in an abstract reasoning test. There are likely to be more rules with the later items, that is, they will become more difficult. So, as you manage your time in such tests, try to be aware of that.
- As the rules can be quite different for different items, do not assume that an earlier rule will apply.

This will be especially important in a later item that resembles an earlier one (see the example in Figure 3.4). Also, there is probably more temptation to persist with a difficult item with abstract, spatial and mechanical items than with verbal or numerical ones. This can obviously mean that your time will not be well-managed. Bearing in mind what has been said about different rules applying to different items, this may mean in any case that you are straining to understand a rule that is not used later in the test.

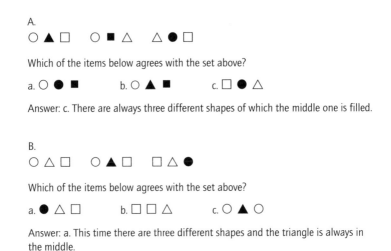

A.

○ ▲ □   ○ ■ △   △ ● □

Which of the items below agrees with the set above?

a. ○ ● ■   b. ○ ▲ ■   c. □ ● △

Answer: c. There are always three different shapes of which the middle one is filled.

B.

○ △ □   ○ ▲ □   □ △ ●

Which of the items below agrees with the set above?

a. ● △ □   b. □ □ △   c. ○ ▲ ○

Answer: a. This time there are three different shapes and the triangle is always in the middle.

Figure 3.4 Abstract reasoning – same shapes, different rules

Spatial and mechanical tests

In these tests the items typically involve two and three dimensional figures and you are asked to interpret them in various ways. Although some of the figures are, again, abstract shapes the task involves reasoning in terms of the spatial aspect, rather than determining patterns in sets as in the abstract items (see Figure 1.1) There are other spatial tests in which the materials are actually three dimensional, such as blocks, rather than two or three dimensional representations on the printed page or screen. Such tests are quite commonly used in the educational assessment of children, but there are a few in place for adults.

Sometimes these tests involving abstract shapes are used in connection with making a general assessment of intelligence, which is discussed below under IQ tests. In other cases they are used where there is a particular need to understand the candidate's spatial awareness. In a recent case a local authority was interested in how well candidates for a director-level post in planning and environment would be able to visualise the built environment. This was seen as particularly important, as much of the area covered by the authority involved high-rise and high value commercial property.

In tests of mechanical comprehension the items are diagrammatic representations of various bits of apparatus or machinery. They are used to assess understanding of the relationships between the different parts of the assemblies represented (see Figure 3.5).

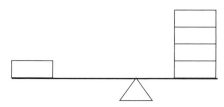

Which way will the right hand of the plank tip?

Answer: Down, the increased number of blocks more than compensates for the shorter distance.

Figure 3.5 Mechanical reasoning example

In general you are far less likely to come across spatial reasoning tests than verbal or numerical ones, unless you are applying for work or training where a good spatial sense is a very definite requirement. This is discussed further in Chapter 9.

Clerical tests

There are several tests available for testing clerical abilities and you may encounter these if you are applying for a clerical support position. Although, like most of the other tests, they are timed, the principle behind them is that they measure accuracy.

This is important in many clerical tasks, from taking down a phone number to entering product codes on order forms. It is an ability that may be looked for in 'paper factories', such as government departments responsible for issuing documents to large sections of the population. Although first photocopiers and then computers have taken on many of the tasks involved, there are still large areas involving a human interface with the computer and many still involving the use of paper forms. Accurate clerical support is also required by many managers, who may have little eye for detail themselves, such characteristics being only rarely (if at all) specified for them.

Examples of clerical test items are shown in the Brilliant Example overleaf. What is the best way of tackling them? One thing to bear in mind is that you will not be faced with complexity, just a series of similar, quite simple, items.

brilliant tip

If you can manage your time to allow for checking of your work at the end you will probably do better than if you go very slowly, as you will then probably be better able to concentrate on items of which you were unsure.

Use the example given in Appendix 2 to get a feel for the pace of working that will give you the best speed versus accuracy trade-off.

 **example**

Clerical test

A retail operation is in the process of putting all of its stock codes onto a computer. The old codes contain a mix of upper and lower case letters and numbers of varying lengths. The computer system needs all of the letters to be upper case and it also requires that for any number sequence with more than four digits a"/" is inserted after the third one. An initial list has been drawn up for computer entry and your task is to check it for accuracy. Mark on the sheet provided any codes that are incorrect. Note that the computer list has been put in alphabetical order.

Manual list	Computer list
AXL428	AXL428
PJZ815	PJZ815
TKR1523	CKX1568
lbd054	LBD054
CKX1568	NPD184/319
tdr178943	PJZ815
BCX430	TDR1789/43
Npd185319	TKR152/3

Other tests of specific abilities

There are various tests of other specific abilities, which you may come across from time to time, but they do not form a regular part of the occupational psychometric scene. They include some further tests in formats other than paper and pencil and their computer-based equivalents. For example, there are a number of tests that involve listening, including tests of comprehension where passages of prose are read out and then candidates have to answer questions about what has been said. Thus these are rather similar to some of the written verbal reasoning tests. There are other listening tests where judgements have to be made about the mood of a person in a recording. One example of these has been used in sales training, where it was employed to help budding salespeople to understand how well they listened to their clients and prospects. Those who did not do well were given remedial support and were re-tested at the end of the course. The same or similar tests could also be used for sales *selection*.

There is little preparation to recommend if you anticipate such tests, apart from making sure that you do get an adequate briefing as the format may be quite unfamiliar to you.

Multitask tests

There are some tests which are designed to measure a number of abilities related to a particular occupation in a single battery. In fact the clerical tests described above could be seen as falling under this heading, although they are often applied separately. In the Computer Programmer Aptitude Battery, on the other hand, all of the tests were assembled in a single booklet and were designed to be administered as a whole. It included tests of numerical and verbal reasoning as well as one on the comprehension of computer flow charts. This particular test now appears to be out of print, possibly as a result of the job of computer programmer having changed. Current tests of computer programming contain items representing numerical and verbal items and the preparation for them is the same as indicated for those above.

So what is IQ?

IQ stands for 'intelligence quotient'. It arose in the early days of testing in the educational field and indicates a person's overall intelligence compared with that of others. It used the idea of mental age compared with actual age. So, if you had a mental age higher than your actual age, you would be seen as more intelligent – having a higher IQ – than the average and vice versa. The comparison was expressed as a percentage. For example a child with a mental age of 10, but an actual age of 8 would have an IQ of $\frac{10}{8} \times 100 = 125$.

Someone with a mental age of 8 at age 10 would have an IQ of $\frac{10}{8} \times 100 = 80$.

A 10-year-old with a mental age that matched their actual age would have an IQ of $\frac{10}{10} \times 100 = 100$.

This idea worked reasonably well for youngsters up to some way into secondary schooling, but it was realised early on that it broke down for adults, the subjects of occupational testing. Thus, given that a person's actual abilities tend not to increase after age 18, the classic reporting of IQ would show deterioration thereafter. So, for an 18-year-old typical of the comparison group, the IQ would be $\frac{18}{18} \times 100 = 100$.

However, for the same person at 36 the IQ on this basis would show as $\frac{18}{36} \times 100 = 50$, for the same test performance.

In fact, rather than making reference to actual age, IQ is now calculated by direct reference to the norm group. So the 36-year-old's performance would be compared to that of other adults and they would show as typical. The actual calculation made is to all intents and purposes a variation of that used to reach a percentile score. However, that can be converted to a scale with 100 as the average, and that is done perhaps out

> IQ is now calculated by direct reference to the norm group

of deference for or continuity with the IQ tradition. Tests used to measure IQ are a mix of various types, including verbal, numerical and abstract. Yet the term is rarely used in occupational testing, where the focus tends to be on specific abilities expressed in percentile terms.

There are, though, a number of books on the market aimed at letting people assess their IQ. They may be of interest in helping you locate your overall mental ability relative to that of others. They are, of course, yet another source of practice items in the numerical, verbal and abstract fields.

Cut-offs

The use of norms means that a cut-off can be applied to an ability test. This may be done to screen people out. For example, the recruiting organisation may decide to use the 30th percentile, so anyone scoring below that would not be passed through to a later stage of the recruitment process. This is quite commonly done in high volume recruitment situations, such as graduate selection or for entry to the military. Where the tests are used at a later stage, say after shortlisting a cut-off may still be applied, but this is far less common. It is more usual to use an ability test score to choose between candidates who were otherwise seen as equivalent.

Other approaches to ability

Some of the other testing methods covered in Chapter 7 have ability components to them, but they also measure aspects of personality. They differ from the ability measures covered here and the personality measures covered next by being generally weaker in terms of norms and having a structure that does not consist of a series of items.

Sample tests

Note that for the numerical tests you will need a calculator. There are two tests each of verbal and numerical reasoning and in each case the second is harder than the first. You may well find the abstract reasoning test quite demanding, but remember, these tests are typically used for senior level positions.

 **action**

Clerical test

Instructions

Read each passage and answer the questions which follow it. You have 20 minutes for the 40 items in this test.

Students enrolling in courses in a college are allowed to take two main and two additional courses in their first year. They may opt to take only a single additional course, but then have to continue that in their second year, which they have to confirm. The table shows the course codes chosen by six students, with main courses prefixed by the letter **M** and additional courses by the letter **A**. Where only one additional course is chosen this needs to be confirmed by the student in the second column for additional courses, by entering the letter **c**.

The individual student entries are then reproduced in the items numbered 1 to 6. If the student has opted for one additional course, but not confirmed it, that should be indicated by the letter **x** appearing after the additional course. For each of these, you are asked to choose one of the alternatives given.

Student	Main	Main	Add.	Add.
J. Ames	Mp439	Mf391	Af481	Ar233
N. Gurat	Mp439	Mt118	Ar233	c
L. Kara	Mh224	Mt119	Aj301	c
S. McBride	Mf391	Mq114	Af481	Ar233
F. Ollerson	Mb439	Mq114	Af228	
N. Quaid	Mh337	Mt119	Aj401	Ar328

▶

1 L. Kara Mh224 Mt119 Aj301 **c**

    a. correct   **b.** error in main

    c. error in additional   **d.** error in confirmation

2 J. Ames Mh224 Mf391 Af481 Ar233

    a. correct   **b.** error in main

    c. error in name   **d.** error in confirmation

3 P. Ollerson Mb439 Mq114 Af228 **x**

    a. correct   **b.** error in name

    c. error in main   **d.** error in confirmation

4 N. Quaid Mh337 Mt119 Af228 Ar328

    a. correct   **b.** error in main

    c. error in additional   **d.** error in confirmation

5 N. Gurat Mp439 Mt118 Ar233 **c**

    a. correct   **b.** error in name

    c. error in additional   **d.** error in confirmation

6 S. McBride Mf391 Mf391 Af481 Ar233

    a. correct   **b.** error in name

    c. error in main   **d.** error in additional

A train operator is obliged to reduce the speed of some of its services running between stations A and B due to track problems. It decides to cancel some of its trains, putting passengers on the next available service.

The remaining fast running services are rescheduled to arrive later. A tour company using the service for its customers going on a week's holiday wants to advise them of changes in departure or arrival time. Use the information in the timetable to indicate any changes to the six customers whose original schedule is shown in items 7 to 12, choosing from the alternatives given. Cancellations are indicated as 'Cncl'.

Original		Revised		Original		Revised	
Dep. A	Arr. B	Dep. A	Arr. B	Dep. B	Arr. A	Dep. B	Arr. A
07.55	09.45	Cncl.	Cncl.	14.20	16.10	14.20	16.40
08.35	10.25	08.35	10.45	15.15	17.35	15.15	17.35
09.00	11.20	09.00	11.20	16.20	18.10	Cncl.	Cncl
10.40	12.30	10.40	13.00	17.00	18.50	17.00	19.30
10.55	12.45	Cncl.	Cncl.	17.30	19.20	Cncl.	Cncl.
12.00	14.20	12.00	14.20	18.10	20.40	18.10	20.40

7   John Smith, out on 07.55, back on 18.10.

    a. no change   **b.** out on 10.25, no change back

    c. out on 08.35, no change back   **d.** out on 09.00, back on 14.20

8   Mr and Mrs. Patel, out on 08.35, back on 14.20.

    a. no change   **b.** out on 07.55, no change back

    c. no change out, arrive back 16.40   **d.** no change out, arrive back 17.35

9   Lara Jones, out on 10.55, back on 17.30.

    a. no change   **b.** no change out, arrive back 1 hr. 20 minutes late

    c. out on12.00, back on 18.10   **d.** out on 10.40, no change back

10 Dr. McGregor, out on 10.55, back on 14.20.

    a. no change   **b.** arrive 1hr. 35 min later than planned on way out

    c. planned train back cancelled   **d.** out on 12.45

11 The group from Woodcroft School, out on 09.00, back on 15.15.

    a. no change   **b.** out on 10.40, back on 16.20

    c. back 30 minutes late   **d.** arrive back 20 minutes late

12 Mrs. Cohen, out on 12.00, back on 17.00

    a. a no change   **b.** arrive 30 minutes late on outward journey

    c. arrive 40 minutes late on return journey   **d.** back on 17.30

▶

A company reimburses employees for expenses, but with certain items disallowed, which are queried by a staff member assigned to check expense forms. These are alcoholic drinks (unless a client is being entertained) taxis without a receipt and breakfast (unless the employee has had to leave home before 06.30). For each of the claims below, indicate which have been correctly and which incorrectly allowed or queried. The whole claim has to be correct for it to be allowed.

13 Bill Brewer   £

Gins & Tonics client meeting ACE electronics	10.00
Taxi ACE offices to Riverside Wine Bar (lost receipt)	7.50
Train London to Westhampton, attend course	50.00
Breakfast en route Westhampton (05.50 home departure)	8.75
Batteries for Dictaphone	3.95

Allowed: **a.** right   **b.** wrong

14 Winston Djamena   £

Coffee with team member during off-site	4.00
Hotel Manchester for trade fair (receipt attached)	182.00
Phone call from station to office (mobile dead)	2.00

Queried: **a.** right   **b.** wrong

15 Jessica Tregarth   £

Breakfast on way to meeting in Birmingham	8.60
Taxi Birmingham Station to office (receipt attached)	5.40
Pub lunch, Birmingham (with J. West Birmingham office)	25.86

Queried: **a.** right   **b.** wrong

16 Seth Fromberg   £

Postage from home to client (Waters Ltd.)	5.00
Taxi office to Waters' premises (no receipt)	8.60

Allowed: **a.** right   **b.** wrong

17 Judith Kraft   £

    Pre-lunch wine J. Groves, client   18.00

    Train London to Manchester, trade fair   116.00

    Coffee en route Manchester   3.60

    Taxi Manchester trade fair to hotel (receipt attached)   6.80

    Queried: **a.** right   **b.** wrong

18 Sulamen B'Charl   £

    Taxi, office to station (carrying heavy bags)   12.00

    New memory stick (to replace damaged one)   14.00

    Allowed: **a.** right   **b.** wrong

A garden centre is cutting some of its prices. It is taking 10% off most of its stock and 15% off plants, except those marked with a *, where the reduction is 20%. Items marked ** are to remain unchanged, while those marked † are to go into the 'all at a fiver' bins. Indicate which of the actions indicated are right and which wrong for the items below.

19 Garden hose: reduce by 10%

    a. right   **b.** wrong

20 Hybrid T roses*: reduce by 15%

    a. right   **b.** wrong

21 Fencing**: increase by 5%

    a. right   **b.** wrong

22 Cockroach powder multipack†: sell at £5.00

    a. right   **b.** wrong

23 Potted fuschias: reduce by 15%

    a. right   **b.** wrong

24 Rubber plants*: reduce by 20%

    a. right   **b.** wrong

▶

25 Secateurs: reduce by 10%

    a. right   **b.** wrong

26 Decorative plastic pots †: sell at £15.00

    a. right   **b.** wrong

27 Creosote: reduce by 10%

    a. right   **b.** wrong

28 Hose accessories **: no change

    a. right   **b.** wrong

29 Azalea plants *: reduce by 20%

    a. right   **b.** wrong

30 Wooden trellis sections: reduce by 10%

    a. right   **b.** wrong

X-Ray Airlines have just taken over their rival, Hainault Skyways. The routes are not being changed yet, but the flight numbers are all to be redesignated. All of the X-Ray numbers below 381 are to be changed so that the first digit is now 7, but otherwise unaltered, and all of the Hainault numbers are to be changed to X-Ray numbers, applying the same rule to numbers below 381. Indicate which of the flight numbers in the following chart have been correctly and which incorrectly changed, where no change is required the relevant cell should be left blank.

	Old	New
31	XR297	XR797
32	HS481	XR781
33	XR442	
34	XR552	HS552
35	HS228	XR728
36	HS403	XR403
37	XR242	XR742
38	HS181	XR181
39	XR555	
40	XR382	XR782

31 a. right   **b.** wrong

32 a. right   **b.** wrong

33 a. right   **b.** wrong

34 a. right   **b.** wrong

35 a. right   **b.** wrong

36 a. right   **b.** wrong

37 a. right   **b.** wrong

38 a. right   **b.** wrong

39 a. right   **b.** wrong

40 a. right   **b.** wrong

Clerical test: answers

1 a	**11** a	**21** b	**31** a
2 b	**12** c	**22** a	**32** b
3 b	**13** b	**23** a	**33** a
4 c	**14** b	**24** a	**34** b
5 a	**15** a	**25** a	**35** a
6 c	**16** b	**26** b	**36** a
7 c	**17** b	**27** a	**37** a
8 c	**18** b	**28** a	**38** b
9 b	**19** a	**29** a	**39** a
10 b	**20** b	**30** a	**40** b

 **action**

Verbal reasoning 1

Instructions

For the following words, choose the one from the alternatives given that is closest to it in meaning. You have 15 minutes for this test, which consists of 30 items.

1   dogged

　　a. determined　　**b.** lazy　　　　　　**c.** tenacious　　**d.** ruthless

2   impudent

　　a. cute　　　　　**b.** cheeky　　　　**c.** reckless　　　**d.** childish

3   porcelain

　　a. china　　　　　**b.** crockery　　　**c.** earthenware　**d.** tea service

4   daintily

　　a. carefully　　　**b.** charmingly　　**c.** fastidiously　**d.** quickly

5   scream

　　a. shout　　　　　**b.** screech　　　　**c.** voice　　　　**d.** call

6   famous

　　a. celebrity　　　**b.** notorious　　　**c.** celebrated　　**d.** reserved

7   gulf

　　a. chasm　　　　　**b.** peninsula　　　**c.** river　　　　**d.** lake

8   cherish

　　a. value　　　　　**b.** clean　　　　　**c.** dislike　　　**d.** support

9   light

　　a. heavy　　　　　**b.** illuminate　　　**c.** cigarette　　**d.** open

10 grumpy

　　a. coarse　　　　　**b.** short　　　　　**c.** surly　　　　**d.** angry

For each of the following words, choose the one from the alternatives given that is most nearly opposite to it in meaning.

11 giant

    a. large   **b.** pygmy   **c.** elf   **d.** troll

12 dear

    a. beloved   **b.** elk   **c.** cheap   **d.** costly

13 quickly

    a. rapidly   **b.** urgently   **c.** lazily   **d.** slowly

14 customary

    a. tax   **b.** polite   **c.** regular   **d.** unusual

15 decorated

    a. ornate   **b.** gilded   **c.** plain   **d.** ugly

16 erroneous

    a. trial   **b.** mistaken   **c.** right   **d.** incorrect

17 premium

    a. top   **b.** excess   **c.** charge   **d.** discount

18 drunk

    a. sot   **b.** teetotaller   **c.** sober   **d.** imbibe

19 neat

    a. scruffy   **b.** tidy   **c.** closed   **d.** smart

20 talkative

    a. garrulous   **b.** reserved   **c.** quiet   **d.** wordy

Choose the word from the alternatives given that best fits the gap in each sentence.

21 Ted was small, but very noisy and chatty, so he made his .... felt.

    a. opinions   **b.** presence   **c.** voice   **d.** conversation

22 Had it not been for the .... arrival of reinforcements the battle would have been lost.

    a. general's   **b.** late   **c.** timely   **d.** urgent

23 Martha gave her grandson a .... when he passed his exams.

    a. smile   **b.** present   **c.** certificate   **d.** telling-off

24 I am going to the match too, so would you like a .... in my car?

    a. seat   **b.** trip   **c.** lift   **d.** journey

25 Yesterday was very cold, but I think today will be ....

    a. milder   **b.** hot   **c.** temperate   **d.** forecast

26 We suddenly came upon a breathtaking .... with hills and valley stretching far into the distance and a waterfall plunging deep below us.

    a. climb   **b.** countryside   **c.** plateau   **d.** view

27 I can't say I am keen on modern art as I don't understand it, so give me a traditional landscape or .... any time.

    a. artist   **b.** watercolour   **c.** canvas   **d.** portrait

28 Celebrity chefs are certainly very popular, but it is questionable as to whether they all fulfil their .... to educate as well as to entertain.

    a. role   **b.** recipes   **c.** potential   **d.** vocation

29 Jeff had asked Julie to go clubbing with him, but she wanted to bring her friend Gloria, which meant he had to find a .... to go along too.

    a. chaperone   **b.** mate   **c.** socialite   **d.** rapper

30 The sales of newspapers have gone down steadily since the arrival of other ways of informing people about what is going on in the world, but no-one can say for sure that they won't be .... in another 10 years.

    a. booming   **b.** distributed   **c.** gone   **d.** around

Verbal reasoning 1: Answers

1 c	**11** b	**21** b
2 b	**12** c	**22** c
3 a	**13** d	**23** b
4 c	**14** d	**24** c
5 b	**15** c	**25** a
6 c	**16** c	**26** d
7 a	**17** d	**27** d
8 a	**18** c	**28** c
9 b	**19** a	**29** b
10 c	**20** c	**30** d

 **action**

Verbal reasoning 2

Instructions

Read each passage and answer the questions which follow it. Base your answers on the information contained in the passage. You have 30 minutes for the 36 items in this test.

Health services are increasingly trying to ensure that resources are matched to patient needs. However, they have to do so mindful of national requirements and things like the responsiveness of the condition to the application of resources. For example the eradication of MRSA is a high national priority and also readily amenable to prevention through improved hygiene practices, so should be capable of eradication quite readily. Coronary heart disease (CHD) on the other hand, is a result of a complex of social and environmental factors interacting with hereditary predispositions. Hence its prevention, treatment and overall management involves a variety of resources and bodies not directly within the remit of frontline services.

Detailed weighting schemes are part of the armoury of tools available to the service providers as they seek to improve health. Although they do not contribute directly, the objectivity that they can bring to debates on health resourcing help to focus resources appropriately. However, in the past there have been many health professionals – particularly amongst the ranks of clinicians – who have been antagonistic to such methods, feeling that they compromised their independence of action.

1   MRSA is a serious issue and not just on an occasional local basis.

   a. likely to be true   **b.** likely to be false   **c.** can't say

2   Health services try to focus on patient needs.

   a. true   **b.** false   **c.** can't say

3 Doctors are the least vocal of those who object to the use of weighting schemes for health resourcing decisions.

a. true   **b.** false   **c.** can't say

4 CHD is too complicated to feature on localised resource weighting schemes.

a. true   **b.** false   **c.** can't say

5 Responsiveness to treatment is one of the criteria that has to be used by health services in deciding how to spend money.

a. true   **b.** false   **c.** can't say

6 Health services will sometimes clash with doctors over the use of weighting schemes to decide on the allocation of resources.

a. likely to be true   **b.** likely to be false   **c.** can't say

Archaeology is sometimes seen as an attractive pursuit by people who would find it quite uncongenial in practice. Sitting in front of a TV screen watching the unearthing of a valuable and attractive artefact can give one little feel for the months or years of painstaking work that has led up to the moment of discovery. Working in harsh and uncomfortable climates, breaking through rocks and endlessly sifting through detritus to seek the hidden gem or the missing piece in the jigsaw of a civilisation's history is not for the faint-hearted. And that says nothing of the hours of research in dusty libraries, poring over faint and scarcely decipherable texts that give the clues as to where to look in the first place and negotiating with bureaucrats for the necessary permissions to dig. Howard Carter expended a lot of toil and sweat in Egypt's Valley of the Kings. True, he did discover the Treasure of Tutankhamun – the lost wonders buried with the young pharaoh in his tomb – but it took another two years for him to clear the burial chamber of its amazing hoard.

7 Most people would like to come across hidden treasure without having to work hard at finding it.

    a. true   **b.** false   **c.** can't say

8 Howard Carter had a licence from the Egyptian authorities to dig in the Valley of the Kings.

    a. probably true   **b.** definitely true   **c.** definitely false

9 Archaeological discoveries are sought to help understand past civilisations.

    a. true   **b.** false   **c.** can't say

10 The Valley of the Kings is an uncomfortable place to dig because it is hot and rocky.

    a. true   **b.** false   **c.** can't say

11 A TV programme showing the final stages leading up to a discovery on an archaeological dig can get across what it is like to have been there and to have worked hard to achieve a really exciting find.

    a. true   **b.** false   **c.** can't say

12 Tomb raiders had left next to nothing in Tutankhamun's tomb when Carter arrived.

    a. true   **b.** false   **c.** can't say

Horse-racing has been called the sport of kings, but commoners as well as potentates gain immense enjoyment from it. Lots of people in England will have a 'flutter' – that is, a bet with a bookmaker – on the big annual races like the Grand National at Aintree or the Derby and many of them go to the races on a more regular basis. For rich and poor a lot of fun is had on these occasions. At some race meetings, but especially Royal Ascot, the pleasure is increased by dressing up in fancy clothes, particularly hats for the ladies. It is an expensive matter to own thoroughbred horses and race them, but that cost is often shared by people who get together in a syndicate. Sharing the cost between, say, 10 people in that way saves money and does little to diminish the excitement of seeing the animal perform in a race.

13 The Derby is run at Aintree.

    a. true   **b.** false   **c.** can't say

14 Syndicates that own racehorses usually consist of 10 people.

    a. true   **b.** false   **c.** can't say

15 When placing a bet you must tell the bookmaker that you are having a flutter.

    a. likely to be true   **b.** likely to be false   **c.** definitely true

16 Poorer people who go to the races don't get much enjoyment from doing so.

    a. true   **b.** false   **c.** can't say

17 Bookmakers will take bets on big races from people who don't go to the races regularly.

    a. true   **b.** false   **c.** can't say

18 If you attend Royal Ascot, you can expect to see some ladies wearing fancy hats.

    a. true   **b.** false   **c.** can't say

The internet has been hailed by many as the greatest development in human communication since the invention of printing and some would even say since the development of writing. There is little doubt that it has brought about a dramatic change in how people in the most technologically advanced parts of the world convey ideas to one another and do business. Mass literacy, the telegraph, telephone, radio, TV and film have all been seen as significant steps in facilitating communications. Less recognition is given to some other developments, though, from the metalling of roads to the photocopier and the fax. Yet some have argued that these have been as significant as the more commonly recognised technological advances in the communications field. Few, however, quibble about the primacy that the internet deserves and the fact that it is today the most commonly used means of communication, largely supplanting earlier developments.

19 Railways have been important because they have enabled the rapid distribution of newspapers to a literate public.

    a. true   **b.** false   **c.** can't say

20 A lot of people fail to see the importance of the internet in the communications field.

    a. true   **b.** false   **c.** can't say

21 If you send a fax it is less likely to get the attention of the other person than if you make a phone call.

    a. true   **b.** false   **c.** can't say

22 Many people see printing as an important development in communications.

    a. true   **b.** false   **c.** can't say

23 Fewer fax machines have been sold since the internet became very popular.

    a. true   **b.** probably true   **c.** false

24 Some people recognise nothing other than the development of writing as of more importance in communication than the internet.

    a. true   **b.** probably true   **c.** false

The attractive market town of Garderbridge has seen many changes over the years. Fortunately for its population and the many visitors who go there every year the planners of the 1960s did not interfere with the historic centre of the town to anything like the extent that other parts of the West Country suffered and which makes them unpopular with tourists. The cobbled streets round Market Cross and the attractive parkland running from St. Ninian's Priory all the way down to the river remain largely unaltered in appearance. In fact, the major changes to the structure of the town have affected the parts to the north of the centre where the Victorian terraces have given way to well laid out estates of housing of different sizes, from low rise maisonette blocks to executive homes. Though the appearance of these estates is much different from what was there before and very much in contrast to the historic centre, the quality of building is good. The provision of local shops, schools and community facilities, plus the excellent bus service 'into town', has allowed the estates to develop their own sense of place, while enabling the residents still to feel wholly Garderbridgian.

But the town centre itself is no moth-balled relic. The use of the buildings includes both 'ye olde' eateries and antique shops that one might expect from the age and heritage of the locality, but also everything from internet cafes to wholefood outlets and a Scandinavian furniture store. There is also the attractive Garder Theatre, just a room over the ancient Garder Inn, but it seats 70 and offers excellent productions.

25 While the northern part of Garderbridge is quite pleasant, the southern part is racked by vandalism.

    a. true   **b.** probably false   **c.** can't say

26 Some places in the West Country suffered from changes introduced in the 1960s.

    a. true   **b.** false   **c.** can't say

27 There are few or no Victorian terraces to the north of the centre.

    a. true   **b.** false   **c.** can't say

28 Garderbridge attracts more visitors than a number of other towns in the region.

    a. true   **b.** false   **c.** can't say

29 People come to Garderbridge particularly to buy antique Scandinavian furniture.

    a. definitely true   **b.** probably false   **c.** definitely false

30 There are no longer monks at the priory.

    a. true   **b.** false   **c.** can't tell

Following Jane Doe's departure next month we shall need another building security co-ordinator. The duties are not onerous, but they are important. Principally they involve maintaining a schedule of staff members responsible for opening and closing the offices each day, including switching off the alarms in the morning and re-setting them at night. In the past it has usually worked best to have one person scheduled for each week, but this is not mandatory. The sales team are out of the office a lot and so it is not feasible to include them in the rota. However, they are the ones more likely to be working late than others and, in those circumstances, do the locking up and alarm setting in the evening.

The role also includes briefing newcomers on the procedures, organising the routine alarm testing and evacuation and liaising with the security providers in case of any unusual happenings. The least attractive part is being the person on call if the alarm goes off in the middle of the night, or at the week-end, but you are allowed to come in by taxi if that happens. It only happened once last year and actually Jane was on holiday at the time so Charlie, who was her designated deputy, came in. So yes, we also need a deputy to ensure holiday and sickness cover. Volunteers for that one too please.

Geoff McKeown, Office Manager

31 Opening and closing the office has to be done by the same person over the course of a week.

  a. true   **b.** false   **c.** can't say

32 Jane was glad that she missed having to come in when the alarm went off out of hours.

  a. true   **b.** false   **c.** can't say

33 The alarms are only tested if they have gone off out of hours.

  a. true   **b.** definitely false   **c.** probably false

34 Charlie volunteered to be deputy co-ordinator, but now wants to relinquish that role.

  a. true   **b.** probably true   **c.** false

35 The sales team never come in early.

    a. true   **b.** false   **c.** can't say

36 The alarm often goes off when it shouldn't.

    a. true   **b.** false   **c.** can't say.

Verbal reasoning 2: Answers

1 a. likely to be true: MRSA is referred to in terms of high national priority.

2 a. true: this is made clear in the first sentence.

3 b. false: clinicians are described as being particularly antagonistic.

4 c. can't say: we know that CHD is complicated, but not if it is too much so to feature.

5 a. true: this is clearly stated in the second sentence.

6 a. likely to be true: this is suggested by the clinicians' antagonism.

7 c. can't say: it might be true, but there is nothing in the passage directly about this.

8 a. probably true: getting permission is indicated as something that archaeologists have to do and he was evidently working in the Valley for some time.

9 a. true: the third sentence describes this.

10 c. can't say: one may know that to be a fact, but there is nothing about it in the passage.

11 b. false: the second sentence makes the opposite point.

12 b. false: it took Carter two years to empty it.

13 c. can't say: there is nothing in the passage to say where it is run.

14 c. can't say: 10 people is given as an example, but it is not clear if this is a typical figure or not.

15 b. likely to be false: 'flutter' is put in quotation marks, suggesting that it is used as a slang term here.

16 b. false: both rich and poor are described as having fun.

17 a. true: this is described in the second sentence. ▶

18 a. true: this is referred to in the sentence about Royal Ascot.

19 c. can't say: there is nothing about railways in the passage.

20 c. can't say: many people hailing its importance could still leave a lot who don't see that.

21 c. can't say: nothing has been said about the attention-getting characteristics of any of the media mentioned.

22 a. true: this is clearly indicated in the first sentence.

23 b. probably true: the internet is described as having largely supplanted earlier developments.

24 b. true: this is stated in the first sentence.

25 c. can't say: nothing is said about the southern part at all.

26 a. true: this is stated in the second sentence.

27 a. true: they are described as having been replaced by the new estates.

28 a. true: this is indicated in the second sentence.

29 b. probably false: there are antique shops and there is at least one Scandinavian furniture shop, but the two have not been linked and the town is described as having other charms.

30 c. can't tell: we aren't told anything about the priory.

31 b. false: this is described as usual, but not mandatory.

32 c. can't say: we don't know if she was bothered or not.

33 b. definitely false: they are described as being tested routinely.

34 b. probably true: volunteers are being asked for now, so the post of deputy is open and it would be likely that the same processes would have been used last time round.

35 c. can't say: we are not told anything about whether or not they ever arrive early.

36 b. false: it only did so once in the last year.

 **action**

Numerical reasoning 1

Instructions

Select the correct answer from the alternatives given below. You have 20 minutes for this test.

1 83 – 17

   a. 66   **b.** 47   **c.** 56   **d.** 100

2 23×9

   a. 221   **b.** 207   **c.** 270   **d.** 217

3 118 + 259

   a. 377   **b.** 141   **c.** 587   **d.** 357

4 $\frac{242}{11}$

   a. 32   **b.** 22   **c.** 31   **d.** 42

5 232 + 457

   a. 717   **b.** 691   **c.** 689   **d.** 225

6 $\frac{3}{5} - \frac{7}{15}$

   a. $\frac{2}{5}$ **b.** $\frac{4}{15}$ **c.** $-\frac{1}{15}$ **d.** $\frac{2}{15}$

7 2.5×12

   a. 3.0   **b.** 30   **c.** 28   **d.** 25

8 1.8 – 7.2

   a. 9   **b.** 54   **c.** –5.4   **d.** –5.6

9 1,038 – 39.41

   a. 99.59   **b.** 999.58   **c.** 998.59   **d.** 630.49

10 Subtract 2.5% from 98

   a. 95.55   **b.** 95.50   **c.** 97.50   **d.** 9.75   ▶

11 What per cent of 144 is 36?

    a. 2.8   **b.** 25   **c.** 33.3   **d.** 28

12 How many 30 centilitre bottles can be completely filled from a 100 litre container?

    a. 300   **b.** 3,000   **c.** 330   **d.** 333

13 What fraction of 343 is 7?

    a. $\frac{1}{50}$ **b.** $\frac{1}{49}$ **c.** $\frac{2}{83}$ **d.** $\frac{1}{51}$

14 What is the average speed of a runner who travels 2.5 miles in half an hour and 1.6 miles in the next half hour, in miles per hour?

    a. 2.05   **b.** 2.80   **c.** 1.85   **d.** 2.00

15 If the price of a railway ticket goes up by approximately 10% to stand at £45, what was it before?

    a. £40.5   **b.** £40.00   **c.** £40.90   **d.** £39.50

16 What number comes next in the series 2, 4, 8, 32, 256?

    a. 512   **b.** 820   **c.** 8,192   **d.** 524,288

17 What number comes next in the series 1, 5, 3, 7, 5, 9

    a. 11   **b.** 7   **c.** 5   **d.** 15

18 What number is missing from the series 1, 8 . . . 64, 512

    a. 4   **b.** 16   **c.** 8   **d.** 256

19 What number is missing from the series 9, 16, 25, 36 . . . 64

    a. 7   **b.** 48   **c.** 51   **d.** 49

20 What number is next in the series 256, 243, 112, 81, 56 . . .

    a. 27   **b.** 28   **c.** 9   **d.** 48

21 If VAT is reduced from 15% to 11% on an item costing £12 total, what is the new price?

    a. £12.48   **b.** £11.48   **c.** £11.52   **d.** £10.52

22 If 12.5% service has been added to a restaurant bill that comes to £154 altogether, what was the original total?

  a. £141.50   **b.** £136.89   **c.** £134.99   **d.** £134.75

23 What is the average speed of a barge which travels 3 km in half an hour and 2 km in the next quarter of an hour?

  a. 5 kph   **b.** 6 kph   **c.** 7 kph   **d.** 4 kph

24 If an energy-saving bulb uses a quarter of the electricity of a regular bulb each hour but is twice as expensive to buy, how long will it take to repay its cost?

  a. 60 hours   **b.** 4 hours   **c.** can't say   **d.** will never catch up

25 If a shop reduces the prices on goods that account for 60% of its sales by 5% and on the rest by 10% and sells exactly the same number of each item as before, by how much will the value of its sales have dropped?

  a. 7%   **b.** 7.5%   **c.** 15%   **d.** 8%.

26 If increasing the speed of a car from 60 to 70 mph results in a 15% increase in fuel consumption and a driver drives for half an hour at 70 mph and three hours at 60 mph on part of a journey, how much more fuel will they use than if they drove at 60 mph for the whole of that part of the journey?

  a. 3.2%   **b.** 2.14%   **c.** 13.5%   **d.** 1.18%

27 If a passenger tells a taxi driver to keep the change when they give them a £20 note for a fare of £18.36, what percentage is their tip?

  a. 10.1%   **b.** 8.9%   **c.** 8.0%   **d.** 8.2%

28 How long will it take a 100 litre container to empty if 5 litres are taken out in 1 minute in a bucket and the rest is let out through a tap at the rate of 2 litres per minute?

  a. 53 min 30 secs.   **b.** 52 min 30 secs.   **c.** 1 hour   **d.** 47 min 30 secs.

▶

29 If a traveller flies 3,000 miles across the Atlantic in 7 hours, but spends
2 hours in taxis at either end to cover 40 miles in total plus 3 hours at
the airports, what is their average journey speed door to door?

   a. 253 mph   **b.** 553 mph   **c.** 428 mph   **d.** can't say.

30 If there are 12 Ruritanian crowns to the pound, but the pound then
drops by 10%, what is a crown now worth?

   a. 8.5p   **b.** 9.26p   **c.** 13p   **d.** 80p

Numerical reasoning 1: Answers

1	a. 66	**16**	c. 8192
2	b. 207	**17**	b. 7
3	a. 377	**18**	c. 8
4	b. 22	**19**	d. 49
5	c. 689	**20**	a. 27
6	d. $\frac{2}{15}$	**21**	a. £11.58
7	b. 30	**22**	b. £136.89
8	c. −5.4	**23**	c. 7 kph
9	c. 998.59	**24**	c. (can't say − don't know cost of bulbs)
10	b. 99.5	**25**	a. 7%
11	b. 25	**26**	b. 2.14%
12	d. 333	**27**	b. 8.9%
13	b. $\frac{1}{49}$	**28**	d. 48 min 30 sec.
14	c. 4.1	**29**	a. 253
15	c. 40.9	**30**	b. 92.6p

 **action**

Numerical reasoning 2

Instructions

You have 35 minutes to answer the following 30 questions.

The table below shows UK population figures.

	2001	2005	2011	2021
		Millions		
England	49.4	50.4	52.0	54.6
Wales	2.9	3.0	3.0	3.2
Scotland	5.1	5.1	5.1	5.1
N. Ireland	1.7	1.7	1.8	1.8
UK	**59.1**	**60.2**	**61.9**	**64.7**

Percentages are rounded to the nearest whole decimal point.

1 By what percentage is the UK total population expected to grow between 2005 and 2021?

   a. 7.0   **b.** 7.5   **c.** 4.7   **d.** 4.5

2 In which part of the UK did the population grow by 100,000 between 2001 and 2005?

   a. N. Ireland   **b.** Scotland   **c.** England   **d.** Wales.

3 What is the expected percentage growth in population in Northern Ireland between 2005 and 2021?

   a. 0   **b.** 1.0   **c.** 5.9   **d.** 5.6

4 Which part of the UK is expected to see the highest percentage population growth between 2001 and 2011?

   a. England   **b.** Wales   **c.** Scotland   **d.** N. Ireland

5 By what percentage is the population of Wales, Scotland and N. Ireland expected to grow between 2005 and 2021?

  a. 3.1   **b.** 32   **c.** 2.8   **d.** 3.0

The chart below shows the forecast (◊) and actual (□) maximum daily temperatures in °C for a five-week winter period.

	Week 1	Week 2	Week 3	Week 4	Week 5
8					
7	◊		◊		
6	□	◊		◊	◊
5					
4		□			
3			□	□	
2					□
1					
0					

6 What is the average discrepancy between the actual and forecast temperatures?

  a. 3.9°   **b.** 5.0°   **c.** 2.8°   **d.** 2.0°

7 How many times greater is the discrepancy between the actual and forecast temperatures comparing the least and most accurate forecasts?

  a. 3 times   **b.** 4 times   **c.** 2.5 times   **d.** 6 times

8 If the temperature in Week 6 were forecast to be 3°C and was an overestimate by the same amount as in Week 2, what would be the actual temperature in Week 6?

  a. 0°   **b.** 5°   **c.** 1°   **d.** 2°

9 If a new forecast is made for Week 3 onwards, which improves the accuracy by one degree for each week, what will have been the average forecast temperature over the five-week period?

   a. can't say   **b.** 5.8°   **c.** 5.4°   **d.** 2.7°

10 If the forecast temperature had been 3° less in each of the five weeks, what would have been the average discrepancy between the actual and forecast temperatures, not taking account of whether the forecast was above or below the actual temperature?

   a. 1°   **b.** −.2°   **c.** 3°   **d.** 0.9°

The diagram below shows the layout of a warehouse belonging to the Kidsfun Toy Store. Distances are in metres, not to scale. The grey area is the trolley pathway.

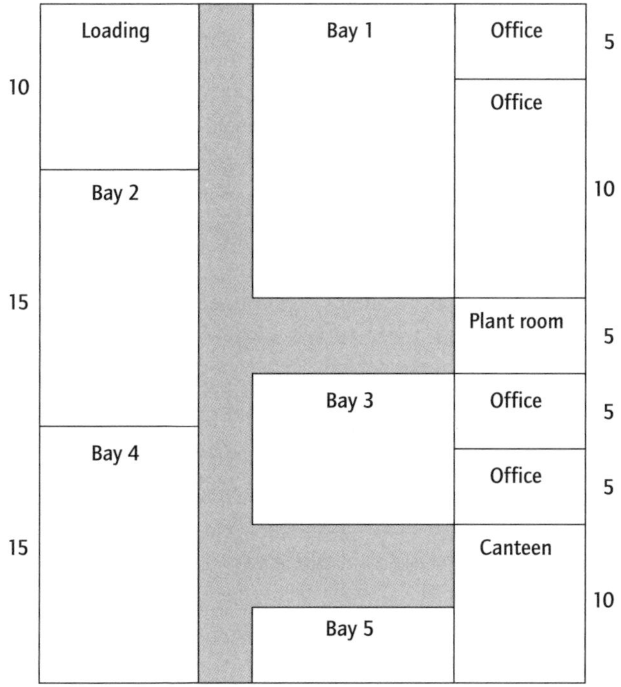

11 What is the total area devoted to offices?

   a. 400 sq.m.   **b.** 225 sq.m.   **c.** 25 sq.m.   **d.** 250 sq.m.

12 New regulations require that the trolley path is at least 4 m wide. If bays 2 and 4 were left alone, what would be the resulting area of Bay 3?

   a. 200 sq.m.   **b.** 1,900 sq.m.   **c.** 190 sq.m.   **d.** 60 sq.m.

13 If the canteen were dispensed with and a quarter of the space were added to the office next to it, with the rest being added to Bay 5, by what percentage would the total office space have been increased?

   a. 50 %   **b.** 5%   **c.** 25%   **d.** 10%

14 If the trolley pathway were increased to be 5 m wide, except in the part next to the loading area, what area would it cover?

   a. 280 sq.m.   **b.** 380 sq.m.   **c.** 290 sq.m.   **d.** 200 sq.m.

15 How much bigger are Bays 2 and 4 combined than Bay 1?

   a. 150%   **b.** 180 sq.m.   **c.** 150 sq.m.   **d.** can't say

The table below shows the increase or decrease in sales figures in £'000s for a group of salespeople quarter by quarter, compared with their individual performance in the previous year.

Salesperson	Q1	Q2	Q3	Q4
John	+10	+15	+11	+20
Ahmed	−5	+5	+30	+40
Lee	+7	−30	−16	+30
Moira	+5	+6	+4	+8
Pierre	+10	−18	+16	+20

16 How much more did Ahmed sell in Q4 last year than Moira in the same quarter this year?

   a. £32,000   **b.** £3,200   **c.** can't say   **d.** both sold the same

17 If Pierre sold £200,000 in Q3 this year, what did he sell in Q3 last year?

   a. can't say   **b.** £216,000   **c.** £180,000   **d.** £184,000

18 If John and Lee each sold £150,000 in Q1 and Q2 last year and then £175,000 in Q3 and Q4 in the same year, in which quarter this year were their sales figures closest to one another's?

   a. Q1   **b.** Q2   **c.** Q3   **d.** Q4

19 If a bonus is given to the salesperson with the highest increase in their sales over the previous year, but John doesn't qualify because he has been promoted, who will get it?

   a. Ahmed   **b.** Lee   **c.** Moira   **d.** Pierre

20 Taking the whole group of salespeople, for the quarters in which an increase in sales occurred, by how much did the figure for the best quarter exceed that for the worst quarter?

   a. can't say   **b.** £140,000   **c.** £91,000   **d.** £18,000

A small private museum and art gallery is reviewing its sources of income, dividing them into the core activities of entry admissions and loans, non-core catering and retail and 'other', which is mainly bequests. The pie chart below shows an overall analysis for the last year and the bar chart gives more detail.

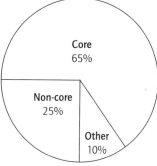

£'000s

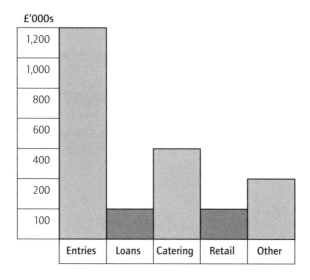

21 How much of the total revenue did loans contribute in the last year?

   a. 5%   b. 15%   c. 8.5%   d. 20%

22 A bequest of £200,000 was received just outside the period covered. Had it arrived inside that period, what would have been the percentage contribution of the 'other' category?

   a. 10%   b. 1.8%   c. 20%   d. 18.1%

23 How much of non-core revenue was contributed by retail?

   a. 25%   b. 20%   c. 15%   d. 10%

24 If the revenue from loans had been half what it was, what would have been the total contribution of core business?

   a. £1.25m   b. £1.2m   c. can't say   d. £125,000

25 If the business changes its retail arrangements next year, to move to a franchise arrangement yielding a quarter of this year's income, how much will non-core contribute in total?

   a. £450,000   b. £50,000   c. £425,000   d. can't say

The North and South Blankshire packaging companies have agreed to merge and are looking at their staffing arrangements, to identify savings. Some, but not all, of their staffing categories are the same. Staff numbers are shown in the tables below.

North Blankshire

Production	Despatch	Design	Marketing	Sales	HQ
82	15	5	6	10	22

South Blankshire

Production	Despatch	Drivers	Design	Sales/ Marketing	Finance	HR	HQ
76	20	5	3	16	6	3	8

26 If half the sales and marketing people were to go and this was spread evenly over the two companies and across sales and marketing, how many sales staff from North Blankshire would be left?

    a. 5   **b.** 7   **c.** can't say   **d.** 8

27 If North Blankshire has the same proportion of drivers to other despatch staff as South Blankshire and two-thirds of them were to go, how many would be left?

    a. 2   **b.** 4   **c.** 10   **d.** 1

28 If three directors and the two office staff who support them go from South Blankshire's HQ as part of the overall deal and the new company is seeking 15% reductions from the combined workforce remaining, approximately how many people will they be looking to lose?

    a. 40   **b.** 22   **c.** 8   **d.** 36

29 If five people each from the overall production, despatch and marketing teams go, how many of the salespeople from South Blankshire will be left?

    a. 11   **b.** 5   **c.** 6   **d.** can't say

▶

30 The North Blankshire HQ team included HR and Finance and three site managers, while South Blankshire's two site managers came under Production. Looking at comparable Production staff, how do the the two companies compare?

   a. 6 more in N. Blankshire

   b. same proportion in each

   c. higher proportion in S. Blankshire

   d. higher proportion N. Blankshire

Numerical reasoning 2: Answers

1	b	11	d	21	a
2	a	12	b	22	d
3	c	13	d	23	b
4	d	14	b	24	a
5	a	15	c	25	d
6	c	16	c	26	a
7	d	17	d	27	d
8	c	18	a	28	a
9	b	19	a	29	d
10	a	20	c	30	d

 action

Abstract reasoning

Instructions

You have 35 minutes for the 35 items in this test.

For each of the following items, choose the pattern from the list of alternatives, a–d, which continues the sequence in the line above.

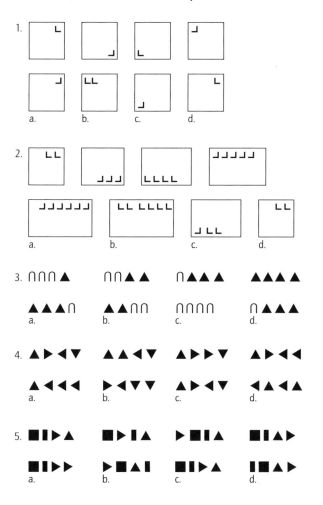

For each of the following items choose the alternative, a–d, which fits in with the set in the line above.

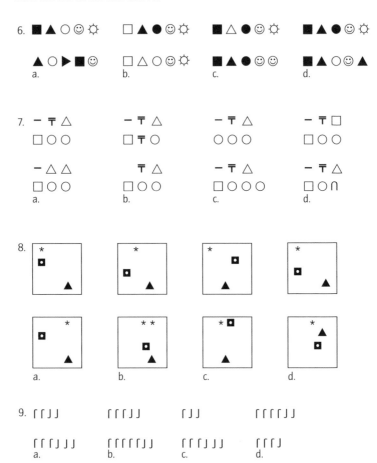

6. ■▲○☺☼   □▲●☺☼   ■△●☺☼   ■▲●☺☼

    ▲○▶■☺   □△○☺☼   ■▲●☺☺   ■▲○☺▲
    a.   b.   c.   d.

7. ─ ╤ △   ─ ╤ △   ─ ╤ △   ─ ╤ □
    □○○   □╤○   ○○○   □○○

    ─ △ △   ╤ △   ─ ╤ △   ─ ╤ △
    □○○   □○○   □○○○   □○∩
    a.   b.   c.   d.

8.

    a.   b.   c.   d.

9. ⌐⌐⌐JJ   ⌐⌐⌐⌐JJ   ⌐JJ   ⌐⌐⌐⌐⌐JJ

    ⌐⌐⌐JJJ   ⌐⌐⌐⌐⌐⌐JJ   ⌐⌐⌐JJJ   ⌐⌐⌐J
    a.   b.   c.   d.

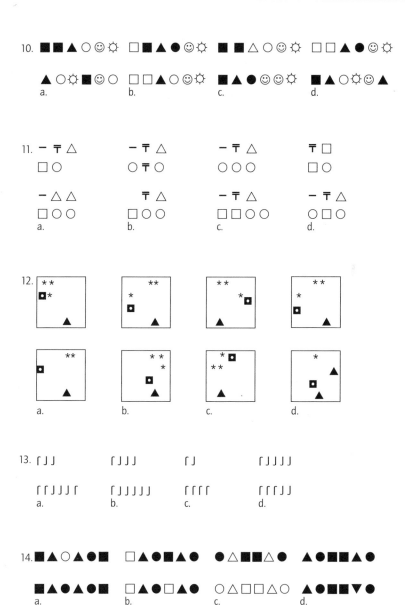

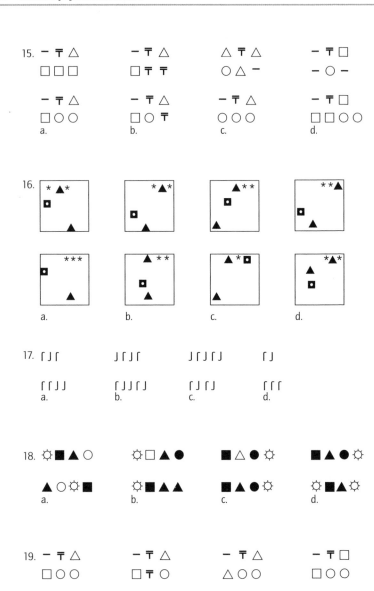

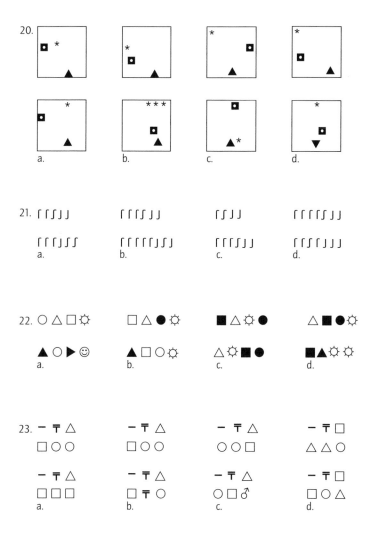

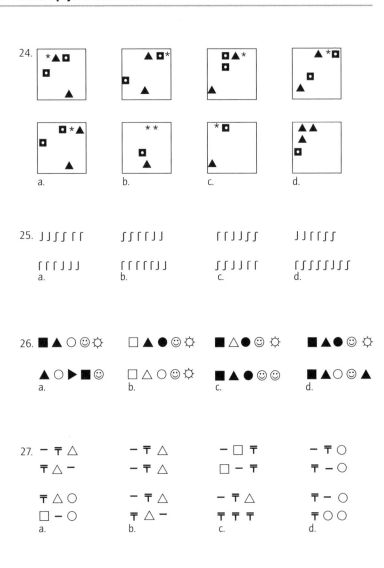

24.

25.

26.

27.

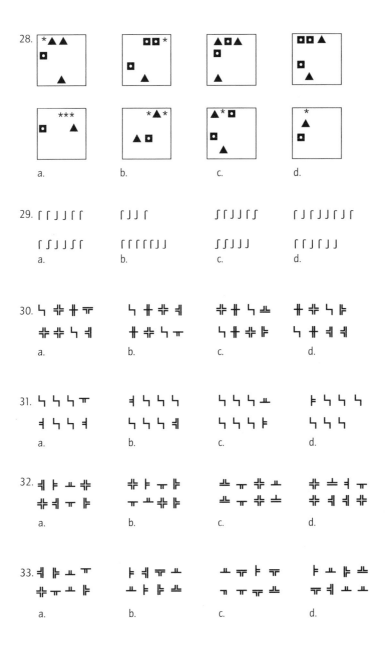

Abstract reasoning: Answers

1   d. The shapes move clockwise and alternate between ∟ and ⌐.

2   b. As 1, but also increasing by one shape each time.

3   a. The sequence moves progressively from right to left.

4   b. Moving from left to right the number of each shape doubles, replacing the original shape.

5   c. The right pointing triangle moves progressively from right to left.

6   b. The small square, triangle and circle always appear first, with the triangle in the middle of the three; they may be open or filled. The smiling face and sun always follow and are always open.

7   a. There are six shapes each time, drawn from the same set. One of those might appear twice each time.

8   a. The asterisk is always on the top row and the triangle on the bottom row. The square may be on the second or third row.

9   b. Two of the ⌐ shapes are followed by two of the ⌐ shapes.

10   b. The square or circle appear first followed by the triangle and the other one of the square or circle. There are two of one of these shapes and they may be open or filled. The smiling face and sun follow and are always open.

11   b. There are six shapes in each group, counting the squares as two.

12   b. There are two asterisks on the top row, one on the second row, a square on the second or third row and a triangle on the bottom row.

13   b. One of the ⌐ is followed by one of the ⌐ shapes.

14   c. The three shapes are repeated, but with variations in order and/or shading.

15   c. There are three of one of the shapes in each group.

16   b. There are two asterisks and a triangle in the top row, a square in the second or third and a triangle on the bottom row.

17   c. The figures alternate.

18   c. There is a square a triangle and a circle, and one sun, which is always at one or other end of the line.

19 a. There are six shapes in each set and at least two of them in any one set.

20 a. In each case there is an asterisk on the top or second row, a square on the second or third row and a triangle on the bottom row.

21 d. There is always the pair ſ ſ.

22 c. The triangle is always open.

23 d. One of the shapes appears twice.

24 a. There is a triangle, a circle and a square on the top row, a square on the second or third row and a triangle on the bottom row.

25 c. There are two of each shape together.

26 b. There is one each of circle, square, triangle, smiling face and sun.

27 b. Each line has the same three shapes.

28 c. There are three shapes in each top line, a square in the second or third line and a triangle in the fourth line.

29 a. The first set of figures is repeated in reverse order.

30 c. One of each of the shapes appears in each set; the ⊣ shape may be rotated.

31 c. There are three ⌐ and a ⊤, ⊤ which may be rotated.

32 b. There is one ⊹, one ⊣, which may be rotated and two ⊤, in different rotations.

33 b. There are two ⊣ shapes and two ⊤ shapes, which may be rotated in each case.

CHAPTER 4

Who are you? More on personality and motivation

Broad brush measures

The personality questionnaires that you will come across most commonly have relatively large numbers of scales. The Sixteen Personality Questionnaire (16PF) defines itself by its 16 scales and the Occupational Personality Questionnaire (OPQ) has 32. In Wave there is a four tier structure, with no fewer than 108 facets at the lowest level. Each of these questionnaires has the scope to produce information on a number of derivative scales, such as a variety of team types, indicating a person's typical role in a team.

Altogether, such personality measures provide a lot of data. The users work with the information in several different ways. Sometimes, it is used to produce a generalised description of the candidate, which may be organised under headings reflecting the way the scales are arranged. For example, for the OPQ the 32 scales are grouped into:

- relationships with people;
- thinking style;
- feelings and emotions.

More commonly the personality measure will be mapped against some of the requirements of the role, which will indicate the scales seen as relevant. Such mapping will be done rather judgementally, but often two or three test users will work on it together. The illustration in the table is based on a mapping exercise using the OPQ. The complete version involved 10 different requirement areas.

Personality mapping	
Requirement	Personality scales
Orientation to change	Innovation, conventional (low to mid), variety seeking, adaptable
Orderly & stable	Detail conscious, conscientious, rule following, emotionally controlled, worrying (low)
Inspirational leadership	Outgoing, socially confident, conceptual, innovative
Problem solving & decision-making	Analysis , decisive (mid to upper-mid)
Focus on results	Achieving, competitive, data rational

The mapping against requirements can be seen as reinforcing the point made in Chapter 2, that personality measures are interpreted in accordance with particular requirements, so that they do function as tests. This is particularly so where the indications from the personality measure are accompanied by ratings. Sometimes the results according to the mapping will be described in the body of a report, with an overview, reflecting the groupings being given in an introductory paragraph or two.

Quite often the part of the report which presents the results according to the different requirements will be followed by a number of questions for consideration by a final panel.

If you think about this rather detailed way in which a report from a broad brush measure can be put together, you may see that it is going to be difficult to second guess how your responses will be interpreted. To do that you would first have to know how the items related to the scales in the measure – quite tricky in itself when there might be, as we have seen, many scales involved. You would then need to understand how those scales related to the requirements of the role. You may have been given a person specification which could give you some clues here, but you won't have had access to the thinking of the people doing the mapping of the scales to the requirements.

brilliant tip

Don't try to represent yourself as other than you are: you are unlikely to do it well and may be caught out.

The big five

Another way that psychometrics looks at personality is by way of the 'big five' model. Those who take this view of personality suggest that it can be reflected in five main factors. These are:

1   Neuroticism

2   Openness to experience

3   Extraversion

4   Agreeableness

5   Conscientiousness

An example of a personality questionnaire using a big five model is the well-established NEO PI-R, published by Hogrefe, Oxford.

The specific labels vary: 'culture' is sometimes used instead of 'openness' and 'emotional stability' for 'neuroticism', i.e. following the other end of the same scale. There are also arguments as to whether there are really five factors or some other number – the 'great eight' is another model.

Some or all of the big five can be worked out from some of the broad brush measures and they may be used in the overall or summary reporting about a candidate, providing yet another aspect you would need to master if you were to 'fake good' effectively. There are other personality measures that concentrate directly on the big five, but with those you could still be tripped up by the feedback process or by the response-style scales (described below under 'Catching you out') should you be tempted to portray yourself as other than you are.

Other models

There are also a lot of personality psychometrics that focus on a specific area. These are used less often than the broad brush or the big five measures, but may sometimes be employed alongside them. They will typically be used not to gain insights strictly related to the person specification, but as part of further rounding out a picture. Sometimes they seem to be used because a consultant has put together a standard package of measures rather than because their relevance can be demonstrated in all cases. For example the Thomas Kilman Conflict Resolution Inventory looks at five different approaches to resolving conflict. It is likely to be helpful in roles in which conflict is to be encountered, but arguably is not universally useful. If you are asked to undertake a measure such as this you might want to establish why it is being used. If it is just part of a standard package you might have reason to challenge its use (for when and how to mount this or other challenges, see Chapter 8.)

Expert system reporting

Sometimes the results of personality measures are presented in the form of an expert system report. There, your pattern of results is looked at by means of a computer program which selects sentences and paragraphs from a 'library' of descriptions produced in advance by people who are expert in interpreting the particular questionnaire involved. This has the potential advantage for you of knowing that you are going through a highly standardised process, building on the systematisation given by the use of norms to produce interpretations of the results that have all been arrived at in the same way. Often expert system reports will also include suggestions for follow-up questions. Thus the variations in details of interpretation that will inevitably arise even with highly trained users of personality psychometrics are eliminated. This means that all candidates are on a level playing field. Variations can arise as a single user looks at different candidates and even more so if more than one user is involved. The use of mapping plus cross-checking and monitoring of reports go some way to eliminating such variations, but will never do so completely. An example of an expert system reports is given in Appendix 2.

One of the downsides of expert system reporting is that it does not provide the scope for reflecting the characteristics for a particular role that is afforded by a report specifically written with the role in mind. Also, I have found that in practice there is a tendency to use expert system reports very much as a matter of expediency and that, among other things, the useful process of feedback, discussed in some detail below, is not undertaken. In fact, there is no reason why feedback should not be given when expert system reporting is used. In those cases the report could be supplemented by notes arising from the feedback, but that does not appear to be done routinely.

Another aspect of expediency is the use of the expert system report as a *basis* for writing a more tailored report. When this is done many of the paragraphs from the expert report are retained, but others are added by the consultant concerned. This would, of course, convey some of the benefits of standardisation, but the argument advanced by those who do this are that it is easier. I have never found that to be the case and invariably want to write the whole report myself, rather than engaging in what I would find to be a rather tedious editorial process, but it is a matter of preference.

As a candidate you may not be told in advance whether or not expert system reporting is to be used. It is unlikely to be of significance to you unless you wish to mount a challenge to the process, which is discussed in Chapter 8.

Catching you out

For nearly every personality measure there is scope for the user interpreting the tests to gain insights on various forms of irregularity in response. These might be as a result of a deliberate effort on the part of the candidate to make a false representation of themselves, or it could be done quite unconsciously and suggest a routine tendency to put themselves in a good light. Other response style indicators flag up patterns of response that are unusual or inconsistent in some way.

The 'good light' indicators are to do with social desirability. The idea is that if you tend to respond in ways that are very largely in line with ideas of socially desirable behaviour, you are likely to have over-represented yourself. Are you really always honest, straightforward, kind and considerate to others, willing to admit when you have made a mistake and prepared to stand up for what you see as right even against seemingly overwhelming odds? If that is you, then you might also be expected to fly and have X-ray vision! So, if that is how you have, wittingly or unwittingly, represented yourself through your response to the

> the 'good light' indicators are to do with social desirability

questionnaire, then you will excite suspicion that there has been some distortion in the picture portrayed.

The items in the personality questionnaire reflecting social desirability are sometimes additional to those for the scales of the questionnaire proper, but will be spread throughout so that their purpose is not immediately apparent. In other questionnaires the social desirability indications are taken from responses to a number of the regular items.

It is worth noting that social desirability scales were for a long time known as 'lie scales', which suggests the seriousness with which untoward indications were taken. Another term which is still sometimes used is 'faking good', which is only slightly less derogatory. (There is more about lie detection, measures of honesty and 'integrity tests' in Chapter 9.)

Of course with a social desirability scale there is also the possibility of revealing yourself as having socially undesirable characteristics. Where this is shown it is usually taken as indicating a rather 'brutal' honesty or a 'they must take me as they find me' attitude. Attention will then be less on the social desirability indications themselves than on those from the scales proper, which might for instance show the candidate to be very uncaring and very set in their ways.

As noted in Chapter 1, making a choice between alternatives is more difficult than producing a rating on a scale. This means that it is more difficult with the forced choice, ranking, approach to present an exaggerated picture of yourself in social desirability terms. For example, look at the choices presented in Brilliant Action overleaf and think about how you would manage it with that item.

 **action**

Choices and social desirability

From each pair of descriptors choose the one that is most like you.

1   **a.** I tend to be well-liked.

 b. I tend to be well-respected for my good sense.

2   **a.** People gravitate towards me.

 b. People defer to my opinions.

The ranking measures do sometimes provide an indication of consistency. So if in the first example in Brilliant Action above you chose a. over b., but in the second one you chose b. over a., and repeated that mixed pattern across a number of items, you would be shown as inconsistent.

As noted in Chapter 1 in at least one measure, Wave, the rating and ranking principles are combined. That means that there is scope for a regular overall social desirability measure (termed 'acquiescence' in Wave), but also for an examination of any differences between the two types of response on individual scales. Such differences are interpreted as follows:

● Rating higher than ranking suggests overstated or overoptimistic view of oneself.

● Rating lower than ranking suggests understated or harsh view of oneself.

Unusual patterns can be of two main types. First, although the different scales of a personality measure are described separately there is some degree of relationship, positive or negative, between them. For example, someone showing as being a 'big picture' strategic thinker would probably not show as being highly concerned with detail. On the other hand, someone who was open to change would also probably be alert to opportunities for making improvements. If your results indicate a large number of reversals of these expected relationships, then that will show as a high score on the unusual patterns scale. This might arise, for instance, if you are genuinely a big picture person and not much concerned with detail, but have endeavoured to respond to questions related to detail-handling as if you were.

The second type of unusual pattern is where the candidate has, perhaps, got fed up with the process at some point and made responses randomly or has arbitrarily used the same response point, say 4 on a 5-point scale, regardless of the question. This will present a confusing picture initially and then more detailed inspection will suggest what has been going on. The advice here is that if you don't take part of a selection process seriously you will be unlikely to be seen as a serious candidate, so don't attempt to 'cherry pick' those parts with which you feel most comfortable.

brilliant tip

Be alert to the fact that your patterns of responses can reveal further information about you, including your response to the whole process. So take the personality questionnaire seriously and be yourself.

Of course people are very varied and there are some unusual patterns that reflect that variety. If you are, for instance, someone who is both 'big picture' and 'detail conscious' – and there are a few captains of industry who fall into that joint category – then your response pattern is likely to be flagged as unusual. But all is not lost: this is where feedback can work to your advantage, as discussed next.

Feedback

It is usual, but not invariable, for feedback to be given to the candidate on the results of personality measures. When this is done it is most common for it to occur before a report is written although obviously this is not the case where an unamended expert system report is used. The purpose of providing feedback is twofold, first as a courtesy to the candidate, who will often find the information interesting and useful. The second purpose is to expand upon and provide further understanding of the information given by the results themselves. This second purpose is achieved partly by asking the candidate fairly simply if the picture given by the results is as expected and probing any differences. It is also achieved partly by asking the candidate for examples to illustrate the results. These ideas are neatly captured in the term 'validation interview', which is applied to the rather lengthy feedback sessions recommended with the Wave questionnaire.

Thus, the feedback interview has some points of comparison with the structured interviews that are discussed in Chapter 6. However, in a feedback interview you will not be asked questions to illustrate every aspect of your profile – the questioning will be selective.

When you receive feedback you may or may not be shown a graph of your results. That will depend on the particular personality measure being used, among other things. If you are shown the results in this way then you may notice that rather than being presented in terms of percentiles, you may see a 10 point scale. This is technically called a 'sten' scale, which is short for 'standard 10'. Each point on a sten scale can be related to a percentile: a sten of 5.5 is the same as the 50th percentile and a sten of 9 is approximately the same as the 90th percentile. Stens from 1 to 3 are usually seen as low, stens from 4 to 7 as mid-range and stens from 8 to 10 as high.

There are several points to bear in mind as you experience feed-back.

brilliant tip

You are not being invited to have a rant about all the things you don't like about psychometrics and how you didn't expect to be sub-jected to such a process given your seniority, track record, gender, race or technical qualifications.

If you feel you do have cause for complaint, then voice it maturely, as discussed in Chapter 8. It is relatively unusual for candidates to be wholly intemperate here, but if you end up – or as a colleague of mine experienced recently – start by shouting at the person giving you feedback, then that is unlikely to go unreported. If the results of the personality questionnaire show you to have a tendency to impatience and aggressiveness, then that indication will have been corroborated. Nor should you think that you can get away with selective aggressiveness, as that is likely to earn you the label of bully. A few years ago a candi-date received part of his feedback from a much younger female colleague of mine and part from me. He was very courteous in the session with me, but reduced my colleague to tears. His per-sonality profile suggested that he was aggressive but hierarchical, which seemed to be corroborated by his behaviour.

brilliant tip

Although there may well be some points in the indications that do surprise you, and you should be prepared to challenge those giving your reasons, in general you need to be careful about trying to pres-ent a different image in the feedback from that portrayed by the questionnaire itself.

The feedback process and the issues explored there are supplementary to the personality questionnaire. There may well be queries on your part about the indications from one or two of the scales, but if you are inclined to question every scale on which you don't seem to have come across really positively, you will lose credibility, or at least the response, 'So why do you think you responded as if you were impatient/risk averse/unsociable (or whatever it might be)?'

This will particularly be the case if you cannot find examples of behaviour to back up your assertion. (Whilst drafting this section I gave feedback to a candidate who appeared relatively low on a scale to do with teamworking. He commented that he was sure that was not right as he always thought of himself as a good teamworker. When asked to give an example of his behaviour to illustrate that, he described a situation in which he had imposed a set of objectives on a team, commenting that people needed to be told what to do. I took this as evidence that the initial indications from the questionnaire had been pretty accurate.)

Also, remember that the questioning process during feedback will involve asking you questions to gather illustrations of the behaviour implied by your responses. There are a couple of points to watch out for here. First, the questions are likely to be quite specific and will be directed to finding out more about your typical behaviour in a particular area. What is not being sought is your general philosophy of management or examples unrelated to the question. Spouting management speak and telling the person giving the feedback why, for instance, performance management is important will be far less convincing than talking about steps that you have taken yourself to carry out performance management. In fact, without a con-

> without a concrete example you may cast doubt on whether you have ever done more than read a textbook

crete example you may cast doubt on whether you have ever done more than read a textbook on the subject, which may in turn raise questions over the validity of the indications from the personality measure itself.

With regard to sticking to the point, if you realise that you have been responding for some time and then feel obliged to ask, 'What was the question again?', you have almost certainly not been doing so! Remember that when a question is asked it is not meant to provoke a further description of your total personality and life experiences to stand in parallel with the indications from the personality questionnaire, but a piece of specific evidence. You may well know if you are inclined to ramble in this way and, if so, you might find it useful to make a written note in a couple of words of the key point of the question and glance at that from time to time to keep you on track. (For example, a questioner might ask, 'You appear from your responses to pay attention to motivating people. Do you do that more by being generally lively and enthusiastic or more by tapping into and working with the specific motivations of different individuals?') A useful written note could be, 'motivation, stimulus versus individuals'. I am not suggesting that you should do this for every question as that would tend to slow the process down rather a lot, but so do responses that wander from the point.

Further, if every question gets a response in terms of how 'good' you are in general, then you are likely to be thought to be either 'over-egging the pudding' or not confident about your natural responses to the questionnaire speaking for themselves. In particular, if this tendency shows alongside indications of exaggeration or inconsistency from the response style scales, it is likely to be reported on negatively or at least as something of a question mark, which is probably quite the opposite of what you intended.

If you have responded to the questionnaire honestly, so that the picture represented is pretty much the 'real you', then you should generally have little difficulty in coming up with relevant examples of behaviour. If you cannot do so, then you will cast some doubt on whether or not that 'real you' has actually been captured. Consider the impression if the personality question-naire indicates that you are highly creative, but you cannot come up with a single example of your creativity!

brilliant tip

In receiving feedback do stick to the question asked and give spe-cific examples when called for. A specific example will indicate time, place and what you actually did.

Occasionally people are stumped for ready answers during feed-back and there seem to be several different reasons for that. Sometimes they are surprised to be asked such questions and that can happen even if it has been indicated in the briefing material, as it should be. (So – and this applies to all aspects of being on the receiving end of psychometrics – do take the trouble to read what you are sent in advance.) Also, some people who have not been in the job market for a while do not have ready examples at their fingertips.

So, what can you do to make sure that you can produce examples when called upon? First of all, just being alert to the fact that the feedback session is likely to call for examples should help. Also, you are likely to be asked particularly about aspects of your per-sonality that show up most prominently. You will probably have some awareness of these, so just give some thought in advance as to how you demonstrate those aspects. Lastly, if you do find you don't have an example immediately to hand ask if you can come back to that point at the end of the feedback session.

 tip

Anticipate that you will be asked questions in the feedback session and have examples of what you have actually done readily to hand.

Ink blots and quick glimpses – 'Why are you showing me those funny pictures?'

Many people have heard of, if not seen, ink-blot tests and even know the name of the author of one of these, Rorschach. (That this is something of considerable familiarity is suggested by the fact that an edition of the popular *Penguin Dictionary of Psychology* had an ink-blot shown on its front cover – the sole illustration in the entire book!) The idea behind these is that respondents are asked to interpret pictures that really have no meaning, so that whatever interpretation is placed upon them reveals something about the person concerned and their characteristic way of behaving. In other words, they provide insights into personality. These tests are one example of a category of measures known as 'projective tests', in that you 'project' yourself onto an item that is ambiguous.

There are various types of materials that are used. Pictures are employed in some while in others the items are verbal. You probably won't come across the Rorschach ink-blots when applying for a job and, indeed, none of the projective tests is very commonly used. One that I have used myself in the past is the Rozenzweig Picture Frustration Test, in which the tendency to feel and express frustration is explored through the candidate's response to pictures of frustrating situations such as being splashed by a passing motorist driving through a puddle.

One type that you might come across is the sentence completion test mentioned in Chapter 1. The way in which you choose to complete, the meaning that you project onto the material, is taken as indicative of your characteristic behaviour. (In fact, some of the sentence completion tests move more into the realm of ability than personality testing as their interpretation looks at things like the level of complexity of the responses made.)

The basis on which projective tests are reported is established by comparison with the responses of those who can be regarded as exhibiting the behaviour concerned. So in principle there is the idea of standardisation. However, the way in which candidates' responses are interpreted is often built up by detailed and painstaking study of many responses.

So what should you do if you are confronted with a projective test? Certainly the idea of responding naturally, emphasised throughout, applies here with added force. That is, if it is hard to 'fake good' effectively with the common type of personality questionnaire, it is next to impossible with the complexities of a projective measure. The person doing the interpretation may have spent years being trained in the particular technique, so it is rather unlikely that you can second guess just how it works on the fly as you make your responses.

Another point that bears repetition is that it is not a good idea to pour scorn on the test that you are being asked to take as you go through it or as you receive feedback. Where a projective test is used it is very likely to be something of a pet technique for the organisation concerned and probably a method that they swear by. So, starting off by challenging how they go about things is unlikely to be viewed favourably.

Motivation – what excites me and can I make the effort to use my skills?

As noted in Chapter 1, motivation is sometimes looked at on its own and sometimes considered as part of personality. The point about having a separate measure seems to be to gain an additional slant on the person and to understand the things that are likely to be important to them. This can then be seen as shading into ideas about values. Another way of thinking of this is in terms of motivation as something that will underpin personality and ability. So what will you experience in a motivational questionnaire? It will tend to have the look and feel of a personality measure and without the titles you might sometimes be hard put to tell the difference. Therefore much of what has been said about the approach to adopt in personality measures applies here, too.

Measures of motivation are less likely to include response style indicators than are personality questionnaires. However, the absence of these should not be taken as an invitation to approach the completion of a motivational questionnaire with the intention of displaying a different set of motivators than those that really characterise you. You may find it more uncomfortable to do that than to falsify a personality measure. Also, irregularities in your motivational profile are still likely to show up and, again, you will be subject to the scrutiny of feedback.

The other way in which a motivational questionnaire can be used is to see if your motivations and your other characteristics are in line. For example, if you appeared from reasoning tests to be quite good at handling numbers, but did not display a commercial outlook in a motivational questionnaire, then doubt would be cast on the

> a motivational questionnaire can be used to see if your motivations and your other characteristics are in line

extent to which you would actually make the effort to apply your numerical ability. Such information can obviously be of use to a potential employer.

Is there, then, any special preparation that you can make if you are asked to undertake a motivational questionnaire? The first thing perhaps, is to make sure that you know when that is on the agenda for the recruitment process that you are to experience. In some cases that will be very evident, with questionnaires having the word 'motivation' in their title. In other cases though, this is not quite so apparent. So if asked to complete, say, the XYZ questionnaire, you might want to ask what it is for. Armed with the knowledge that you are being asked to complete a motivation questionnaire rather than a personality one, how might that affect your approach? One thing is to be clear about the context in which you are responding. For some, but by no means all, personality measures you will be asked to respond with the world of work in mind. For motivational questionnaires it might be a work context, or a broader career context or it might be directed at you in terms of the whole of your life. Be alert to instructions that clarify that and respond in terms of the correct context.

 tip

Don't just go blindly into a situation that might involve a motivational measure: check if it actually does and, if so, the context in which you are meant to be answering.

Presenting the findings – how reports are supplemented

Very often a report from any psychometric process will be supplemented by a further process of elaboration of the findings. Thus it is rare for the person writing the report to find that their work is done once the document has been delivered; there is very often a follow-up process. This may take the form of just a covering note in letter or e-mail form from the author of the report to the recruiting manager or other client representative, or it may be conveyed in a phone call. This follow-up activity is more likely to arise in connection with the complexities that can be revealed when personality and motivation measures are used than with ability tests alone.

It is often the case for relatively senior appointments that the psychometric process is applied just to shortlisted candidates before a final panel is held. The author of the report will often attend at the outset of the panel's deliberations, i.e. before the candidates appear. They will typically be asked to summarise key points arising from the assessment and answer questions on the reports from panel members. These questions may be points of clarification, e.g., 'When you say X is more inclined than most to come up with new ideas, does that mean they don't have their feet on the ground?" Alternatively they may seek to explore ground not covered in the report. Sometimes this may be something quite extraneous, such as 'Do they have a sense of humour?' To which the polite response is, 'That was not in the person specification, so I don't think it is relevant to your deliberations and the XYZ questionnaire doesn't measure it anyway.' On other occasions the further questioning is more relevant, such as, 'As you know we are going through a period of change and, from what you say, they are well able to cope with that, but will they be so effective when things become more settled or will they be impatient for even more change?'

It will often be in this session that the panel decides which of any of the suggested follow-up questions in the report are to be used. All of this points to scope for the psychometrics to play quite an important part in the process, although they are unlikely to be the sole factor in an appointment. The point to note here is that the panel will have a picture of you from the psychometrics and they may be rather nonplussed if they see a very different picture during the panel session. Once again this points to the importance of being yourself when you complete a personality questionnaire.

CHAPTER 5

Computer-based testing – what makes it different?

Remote testing – how to face the online challenge

There is nothing very new about testing people remotely, with a candidate in one location linked to a distant computer system. I remember first coming across that approach in the early 1970s in the USA, where it was routinely used for the assessment of blue collar candidates for work in a factory. What is relatively new, of course, is the way in which the internet has made the delivery of tests remotely much more widespread.

With the management level candidates with whom I deal, over the last few years the expectation has grown that they will all have access to the internet and so all one needs to do is to send them a link to get them underway. In the world of shortlists being decided just a few days before final panels and candidates at the other end of the country, there are advantages to all concerned in being able to deliver tests to them in their own offices or homes. However, there are some disadvantages as well and, as a candidate, you need to be alert to these.

Despite their early origins, computer-based tests have only been regulated relatively recently, with guidelines for their development and use only being produced in the UK by the British Psychological Society (BPS) in 1999. There are still disagreements amongst some experts about what tests it is proper to administer remotely by means of electronic methods, too. Thus some people hold that it is not a good idea to administer ability tests in this way, because of the significance of the lack of control over the testing process as opposed to personality measures.

Halt, who goes there?

Impersonation

One potential issue that can arise with remote testing is that of impersonation. That is, rather than sitting the test themselves, candidates are sometimes tempted to get someone else to take their place. Of course that can also be done where the testing is not conducted remotely. However, it is quite unlikely in situations in which the testing session is held late on in a series of activities that the candidate is required to pass through and where the chances of discovery are high. (So if you, a tall blond person, send along a short dark friend to the testing session, but turn up yourself to a meeting with a panel or worse, to the first day of the job, you are likely to be found out.)

The risk of discovery will, however, be far lower when the testing is done at a relatively early stage of the selection process and where the number of people being tested at one time is high. Supervised testing sessions on the graduate milk round and in connection with government training schemes can see over a hundred candidates being put through their paces in an examination hall or a hotel ballroom. In those circumstances the team of administrators would not know if someone appearing at a later stage of the process, having apparently 'passed' the test had actually been present. There would, though, be a risk that a fellow applicant would have been aware of the deception and reported it.

With remote testing the chance of detection generally is low and so, one would suppose, the temptation is greater. But why would you bother? If you consider that you are not much good at numbers and have a willing friend who is something of a mathematical genius, then you may be tempted to get them to sit the test for you. If the ruse works and you perform satisfactorily on other aspects of the selection process, then you might be offered the job. However, if the use of the reasoning test is a real reflection of the requirements of the role, then you may soon be found severely wanting in terms of numerical ability and so lose the position.

There is a slightly different scenario, in which you consider yourself about average with numbers, but are again tempted to substitute your friend on the grounds that they will do a really first class job and so increase your chances of getting in by beating the average or lower than average candidates. Although you might not be caught out on the job, at least not so quickly, you would still have to be confident that your clever friend was actually going to be clever enough with the particular numerical material presented. (Remember the case in Chapter 2 of the engineers who struggled with the commercially-focused numerical reasoning test.)

One of the ways in which test publishers protect the users of tests from impersonation is by splitting the ability test into two parts. The first part is completed online, but for the second part candidates attend the offices of the potential employer or a recruitment consultant and complete it under supervision. Major discrepancies between a candidate's performances on the two parts of the test would arouse suspicion that a substitution had been effected for the online part and further enquiries would be made. The process of splitting the test in this way also means that if the real candidate's performance was just somewhat lower than that of the friendly substitute, the overall result would be

> major discrepancies between a candidate's performances would arouse suspicion

diluted and so any advantage arising from this subterfuge would be reduced. One of the companies using this approach is SHL, with their 'Verify' system. In it the larger part of the test is taken online, but there is provision for part of it to be subsequently administered (still by computer) in a supervised environment.

Contracts and verification – if it wasn't you doing the test, how can you expect to keep the job?

Some online publishers include an 'honesty contract' with the instructions for the test. With such a contract the candidate has to confirm that they are is actually the person concerned and to acknowledge that if a substitution has been made it could invalidate any offer of employment or lead to instant dismissal if discovered after employment has started. This clarification serves to remind candidates of the significance of being dishonest and, importantly, that the test is a substantive part of the selection process. In fact, obtaining advantage by such deception is a criminal offence.

Substitution and personality measures

A greater proportion of personality than ability tests can be delivered online and employers will probably worry less about substitution for those than for the ability measures. Therefore, you are perhaps more likely to encounter online personality than ability psychometrics.

If you are tempted to substitute someone else for yourself, you might want to consider for a moment why that would be appealing. If you are interested in, say, a sales job and know that you are a bit quiet, certainly quieter than your image of the talkative and outgoing salesperson, then you might be tempted to get a more expressive friend to take your place. You might be more tempted to do this if you know that your friend really is a successful salesperson. You will, of course, again run some risk of detection either around the assessment processes or through not being able to do the job if being talkative and outgoing is what is really required. Again, once detected in a deceit you will be liable to instant dismissal. You would also need to be sure in advance that the attributes your friend possesses are the ones actually required in the particular sales role in question. Also, does he have any negative characteristics, such as not being orderly, on which you might show up better? All round, it is much wiser not to attempt deception!

 **tip**

Don't let anyone else take a test for you or help you with it.

Help, I'm a technophobe!

For some people the idea of taking a test on a computer can be worrying. Despite the apparently all-pervasive nature of information technology, not everyone uses it on a routine basis and anxiety about the testing situation in general can be compounded by anxiety about the use of computers. As indicated in Chapter 2, familiarity with the testing set-up in general is likely to be helpful. The links indicated in Appendix 1 should also assist you.

There are some other things you can do, too. One of the advantages of online testing is the scope to take the test at a time more or less to suit you. Quite often this will be at a weekend or in the evening. However, that does mean that any support you may need, for example if you can't get a link to work, may not be available. This can be frustrating and may mean that your carefully-laid plans of taking the test at your convenience have to be rethought, and result in your not being in the best frame of mind when you do go through it.

So, the first thing to explore when agreeing to take a test out of normal working hours is whether or not any form of support will be available to you in case of problems. Test publishers do not run a 24/7 service of this sort, but you will probably be in contact with the potential employer themselves or with a recruitment firm of one sort or another. The latter, in particular, are quite used to handling communications out of hours and may well give you a telephone number or e-mail address to contact in case of difficulty. Although their help will not amount to the full backup of the psychometric publisher, they may well be able, for instance, to re-send a link if it appears that the original has become corrupted. If you are not offered the details of someone to contact, there is no harm in asking.

Next, think about whether it does actually suit you best to do the test in out-of-work hours, or if you would be more comfortable taking it in the knowledge that there is scope for a full panoply of support mechanisms if needed.

brilliant tip

Think about what time to take an online test really suits you best and try to take it then.

Also, note that although computer-based testing generally offers the option of online completion, it is not the only method of administration. So if you feel that you would really be more comfortable with a friendly administrator to brief you at the outset of the testing session and to provide assistance if the computer appears to be 'playing up' in some way, then ask if you can take the test at the client's or recruiter's offices. This may give you the inconvenience of a special journey, but if it results in your giving the test your best shot it might just be worth it.

brilliant tip

If you feel you would rather have a test administrator around ask if that can be arranged.

Differences in the testing experience

Technophobe or not, there are some differences between computer-based tests and paper and pencil versions which can make for confusion when first encountered. To begin with, whilst with a paper and pencil test you can go back and review previous answers, making corrections where necessary, with computer-based testing the scope for this may be limited to the screen of items showing at the time. This can be disconcerting, particularly with a timed ability test, where you might have been unsure of one or two answers, but did not want to linger too long on them, preferring to use any time left when you had completed the whole lot before returning to review your first attempt. You will do well to check on this aspect before launching into the test as there are differences amongst tests in that respect. If you are in a directly supervised testing situation it should be easy enough to establish that in advance, even if it is not made clear in the on-screen instructions, as the test administrator should know the procedures well enough to advise you. If you are doing the test remotely and out-of-hours, it is another point to think of and establish in advance, as it will be too late once the test has begun.

 **tip**

Find out in whether you can go back and check or correct answers, before launching into the test itself.

Another difference is that computer-based tests, particularly when delivered remotely, do have the annoying habit of crashing from time to time. (As programs for the delivery of tests become ever-more sophisticated this may become less and less frequent, but that may be small consolation to you if you are actually faced with an unreliable system.)

With personality or motivation measures this may be no more than just an annoyance, providing you can get back into the system again. With ability tests the picture is more complicated for you and for the person interpreting your results. If you are able to carry on from where you had left off, you may still have been thrown off your stride and this is likely to have some adverse effect on your performance. (The opposite argument, that you will have been given a helpful 'breather', doesn't hold much water if you have spent a frustrating quarter of an hour trying to work out what has gone wrong before managing to get going again.)

> computer-based tests do have the annoying habit of crashing from time to time

In some cases you might be taken back to the beginning. This may, again, be no more than an annoyance in the case of personality measures, but for an ability test the result could be more serious. Once again, you may have been thrown off your stride and so do less well than if everything had gone smoothly. On the other hand, you may be seen as having had the advantage of extra time. The interpreter of the results will not really be in a position to make a precise judgement, but is likely to report the fact of the disturbance, which may lead to your being given the benefit of the doubt in marginal decisions using the test. Of course, they cannot make any judgement of the effect of the disturbance if unaware that it has occurred. It is likely to be more apparent in the case of supervised administration than remote applications, though a detailed record may be available to indicate a stop and start in the latter case.

brilliant tip

If you encounter any problems or disturbances when taking a test, make sure that those interpreting and using the results know about them.

When taking a test online you will typically be sent a link, usually having been advised in advance that you will be receiving it. You may find that the link is sent from the potential employer, the recruitment company involved or the test publisher and that the actual source may not be quite clear in advance, so do watch out for that. Also, even if what to expect and when is absolutely clear you may find that it gets buried in your spam system. This point is made because candidates are confused from time to time and sometimes claim that they have received nothing, even if a read receipt notification has been received by the sender. Thinking you have not received something that you actually have can be frustrating to you as candidate and may dent your credibility a little.

Your lounge isn't a lab

Tapping away at your laptop with the TV blaring, while you keep an eye on the children, is not the controlled environment which you deserve for test taking. You will probably be told when a remote testing session is set up to take care to be in a quiet situation, without risk of interruption or distraction, but no-one else will be in a position to ensure that for you. Particularly, but not exclusively, with ability measures such disturbances can seriously alter your performance, as the story in the Brilliant Example below.

---

brilliant example

Frances had a client in the media business and, as part of a management development Exercise, asked some 30 of their senior people to take the 16PF5 online. That personality measure concludes with a series of reasoning items, with the author having declared that intelligence was a part of personality. Frances had already spent quite a lot of time with a number of the managers and her informal assessment was that they were clever and quite

▶

independent-minded. She was surprised when she found that they had performed relatively poorly on the reasoning scale.

During feedback, Frances found that a number of them had disregarded the instructions in that they had, variously, broken off to go and meet someone from the station, completed the test whilst eating dinner or done it in the office in concert with a couple of colleagues. The independent-mindedness that she had anticipated was apparent in the results and also in this behaviour, but she was very doubtful about the indications on reasoning ability. Frances was alert to this situation as it was a group of people about whose likely reasoning ability she had some preconceptions. Had it been a one-off case she might well have assumed that she had got a fair enough result from the test, even though the person concerned might actually have been having a conversation with a third party whilst completing it.

So, if you are taking the test remotely do take care that your environment is adequately controlled. The Brilliant Tips below indicate the things to take note of. These are based on what a test administrator would follow if conducting a testing session (as recommended by the BPS), but include some other points that particularly apply if you are taking the test at home or at your own place of work.

brilliant tips

Think about the following points before remote testing:

- Explain to family or flatmates that your privacy and space need to be respected while you are undertaking the testing process.

- If taking the test at your workplace consider what, if anything, you want to tell colleagues about what you are doing. You don't want to be embarrassed by having to think up a credible story on the spur of the moment if you don't want your purpose to be known. You might largely cover this by staying late, but you might just find yourself in the company of one or two others.

- If taking the test at your workplace make sure that you are not infringing any rules set by your employer about the use of their equipment and that you will not fall foul of firewalls or other devices limiting receipt of test material.

- Make sure you have a clock or watch available so that you can check on the passage of time as it may or may not be shown on screen.

- Make sure that you have enough space to work, including room for any rough paper that you might need to use.

- Don't use a laptop on your lap; you will be more comfortable and will probably be able to work faster if sitting at a desk or table.

- If there is a phone in the room where you are doing the testing, make sure that it is switched off or on divert. Also, switch off your mobile phone.

Tell-tale details

Timing and response scales

The response-style indications described in Chapter 4 are, of course, all available to the test user with computer-based testing, but they are also supplemented by others. The most obvious ones are those to do with timing. To begin with, for ability tests there can be indications of the total time taken. This is likely to be more precise than in paper and pencil administration, where it is nigh on impossible with more than a handful of candidates. (Note that test administrators are taught that they should be able to handle up to six candidates at a time.) Also, with a single candidate the administrator will not usually stay in the room throughout the testing session. That means that although they may know in a paper and pencil session if the candidate has finished early, if they see them sitting with pencil down on their return and the candidate reports, 'I finished about 5 minutes ago', they won't know exactly how long was taken. The overall time taken may indicate that the candidate was rushing and, if this were to go hand-in-hand with a pattern of responses concentrated on a single point on the rating scale, could suggest that they were not actually taking the process seriously.

Timing information can also be gathered for individual items and this can show if a particular type of ability item caused more difficulty than others or if the candidate had to wrestle with their decision on the response to make on a personality item. These indications might then be followed up further during feedback. (An interesting testing development using response timing is described in Chapter 9.)

Some tests do not allow you to stop and start, but for those that do this information may be recorded and if you have broken off one or more times, it may throw some doubt on how serious you have been in taking the test. Also, stopping and starting may disrupt your concentration.

 **tip**

Complete each test in a single sitting.

Another aspect of response style indicators and computer-based testing is that they are all produced automatically, so are no trouble to the administrator. For paper and pencil administration the extraction of these indicators can be quite tedious and the temptation is for the administrator or user not to bother. (This is not as it should be, but does happen. When making use of a paper and pencil version of the 16PF some years ago I wondered why it always took me longer to score than one of my colleagues. I discovered that he just did not bother to take the extra five minutes or so necessary to derive the indicators.) So, odd patterns of response are even more likely to be revealed in practice with computer-based testing. They can also show up quickly. This can be helpful if the candidate has not understood the instructions for an ability test as this will be flagged by the system and may be investigated without delay.

Additional scales

It is also the power of computing that makes it quite easy to derive a variety of additional scales beyond those that make up the basic dimensions of any one personality measure. For example, with the OPQ, in addition to the 32 scales in the basic profile, readouts can be obtained on a candidate's preferred role in a team, their leadership style and how they like to be led themselves. For some personality measures there are hand scoring methods available for revealing such scales when using paper and pencil administration. However, they take time and by no means all such possible derived scales

> there are some tests that are administered automatically by telephone

can easily be revealed in this way. Although not all situations will call for this wealth of information to be examined, its availability through the power of computing does add to the picture of you can be shown. Among other things, this complexity adds to the difficulties if you were to be tempted to 'fake good'.

Telephone testing

There are some tests – both personality and ability – that are administered automatically by telephone rather than over a computer link, though of course they are computer driven and digitally recorded. (They do require a touchtone phone, but other types are rather antiquated these days anyway.) This approach to remote testing was more frequently in use a few years ago, when access to a phone was much more common than access to a computer – particularly at home. It is still in use by some companies, so you may come across it from time to time.

The origins of this approach can be found in structured interviewing, covered in the next chapter and also in the field of surveys. As a means of delivering ability tests it is limited because as there is no written material the range and difficulty of reasoning items is restricted. Thus you cannot have long passages of prose or diagrams. As far as personality measures go it may seem more user-friendly than written or screen-based material as it uses the spoken word to pose the questions. However, there are variations in how lifelike the recordings sound.

> don't be tempted to take the test while doing something else

If you are asked to take a test in this way remember first of all that it is still a test, not a casual telephone conversation, so many of the tips about controlling your environment still apply. In particular, don't be tempted to take the test while doing something else, like preparing a meal or, worst of all, driving a car! Above all, make sure that you do listen.

Feedback and computer-based testing

Whether a test is delivered online or in a face-to-face environment, using a computer is likely to make little difference to the way that the feedback is delivered. Although you may have completed the test on your own laptop the results will not typically go directly back to you. Rather they will be made available to the registered test user at the organisation commissioning the testing, either the potential employer or the recruiter working for them. (There are some exceptions to this, for example in forms of test that are designed largely for self-insight, such as learning styles instruments, which will be discussed further in Chapter 7.)

With some personality measures the feedback will include providing you with a copy of the results. If you have taken the test online and the feedback is to be given over the phone, then you will be sent the results as an e-mail attachment. You can of course look at this on-screen, but you might find it more convenient to have a hard copy. If so, factor in the arrangements for printing it off into your schedule.

CHAPTER 6

Structured interviewing

Why interviewing at all?

You may be wondering why a book on psychometric testing has anything at all to say on interviews of any sort. There are really two answers to this. First, there are some interviews that are so highly structured and so carefully developed that they share much with conventional psychometric tests. Indeed a term sometimes used for these is 'Structured Psychometric Interviews' (SPI). The second answer is that, regardless of the details of the makeup, some form of structured interview is very common in assessing candidates, so if you expect to experience psychometric tests, you should also expect to experience these.

You will probably remember that we met a type of structured interview in Chapter 4, where the idea of feedback as a 'validation interview' was discussed. That type of interview was structured around the pattern of behaviour suggested by a personality measure. Conventional interviews will often take a candidate's CV as their starting point and Chapter 7 deals with interviews used in following up performance on an in-basket, a type of written exercise. The structured interviews considered here function as measures in their own right, although they are often used together with other measures such as reasoning and personality psychometrics in paper and pencil form.

Questions and competencies

Structured interview questions usually address specific characteristics relevant to a job, so they share that with many of the ability tests, such as those of verbal or numerical reasoning. However, they do not assess those characteristics directly – you will only rarely be asked to do a reasoning task in a structured interview – but by posing items that explore typical behaviour or performance. So that far they have something in common with personality measures. However, in using a personality measure in that way it is necessary to go through a mapping process, as described in Chapter 4. There is no mapping process in going from the structured interview question to the required characteristics, as the questions tap into them directly.

> structured interview questions usually address specific characteristics relevant to a job

Another term used in structured interviewing and elsewhere in connection with psychometrics, but one not used earlier in this book is 'competency': more generally 'characteristics' have been covered. A competency is defined as 'an underlying characteristic of a person that is causally related to effective or superior performance in a job or role'. So this is something that is more or less permanent. This might be an ability, such as numerical reasoning; a part of personality such as trusting others; a motivator such as achievement drive; or a value such as service to others. Temporary conditions or states such as mood would not be competencies, but values such as fairness would be.

The emphasis in the definition of competency on a causal relation means that there is a link between the competency and the resulting behaviour. The reference to effective or superior performance means that the model being used is all about people doing the job really well. Altogether you might think of competencies as going to the heart of performance linked to success.

More on high degrees of structure – the SPI

Questions in structured psychometric interviews will often call for examples of past behaviour. Others will ask for responses to hypothetical situations, attitudes or typical approaches to issues, as in the Brilliant Example below.

 **example**

The following are Structured Psychometric Interview question types.

Past behaviour

Please tell me about a time when you managed to persuade a colleague senior to you not to do something that you thought was too risky.

Hypothetical situation

Suppose that you discovered a problem at work that was not in your area of responsibility; what would you do?

Attitude

Some people say that if you disagree with a rule you should always question it rather than break it. Others say that if you see that a rule is silly you should just ignore it and then justify your actions later if necessary. What is your view?

Typical approach

How do you usually start to work with new colleagues?

In each case the interviewer will be listening out for a response that fits a guideline. Where your response does fit you will be credited with a '1' and otherwise you will get a '0'. The basis for the guidelines which result in the scores is research to distinguish high performers from average performers in the role concerned. So, in the examples given in Table 6.1 the 'a' responses characterise high performers. The 'b' answers look sensible enough on the surface, but they are not typical of what those high performers say.

Table 6.1 The SPI

Question	Guideline	Response	Score
1. When faced with something new to learn at work, how do you go about it?	Systematic approach.	a. I gather all of the information together and then go through it step by step.	1
		b.I like just to dive in and experience it.	0
2. Supposing you were asked to explain your job to a new colleague; how would you go about that?	Finds out what they know first and tailor accordingly.	a. I would ask them if they have come across this sort of work before, so find out about their own experience and fill in the gaps.	1
		b. I would start with the job purpose and then tell them about what I find most interesting.	0

The scope to assign a credit or not in this way is one of the ways in which the SPI functions like more familiar paper and pencil tests. Those who come across it for the first time sometimes think it is very new, but in fact it has been around for about 40 years. It began with the recognition that high performers have different things to say from the average employee.

Arrangement of questions

Another way in which the SPI resembles a personality measure is that, rather than clustering items on one competency together, they are presented so that successive items reflect different competencies. So, if there are seven competencies, item 1 will be for the first competency, item 2 for the second and so on to item 8, which will again be for the first competency. This means that, as with personality psychometrics, it is quite difficult to latch on to what is being assessed by any one item. This will often be the case even if you, as a candidate, have been informed of the competency model in advance.

This arrangement of items in 'runs' also means that it is possible for the recruiting organisation to get some idea about you as a candidate with a short, 'screening' version of the interview, which will often be delivered over the phone or might be used in mass recruitment situations, such as recruitment fairs for graduates or to select staff for a new leisure complex. For example, again with seven competencies, there might be five questions for each competency. Posing the first 14 questions would give an idea of the chances of a cut-off level being reached on the whole interview and, in fact, a provisional cut-off would be applied to this screening interview. (This would be lower than just being in proportion to the whole. This reduces the chances of wrongly cutting off someone in screening who might do quite well on the whole interview.)

Candidates not reaching the screener cut-off would be eliminated and the remainder invited to take the whole of the interview at a later date. The rest of the interview might again be delivered over the phone or at the potential employer's or recruiter's offices. Thus it would function there rather like the 'Verify' model described in the last chapter and again it would be the whole result that would be examined. The occasion to 'come into the office' for the rest of the interview will often be used to apply other psychometric methods.

Once the interview is complete the total number of questions will be added up and this number will be compared with a cut-off. Remember that the interview will have been developed on the basis of the responses of high performers and so the cut-off will be chosen to help the recruiting organisation find more like their best (see Figure 6.1)

Low	performers		
	High	performers	
0 5 10 15	20 25 30 35	40 45 50 55	
cut-off			

Figure 6.1 High and low performers' SPI scores

Table 6.2 Two candidates

Competency	1	2	3	4	5
Results focus		A			B
Perseverance			A	B	
Detail handling			A	B	
Interpersonal sensitivity	B			A	
Communication		B			
Empowering others	B		A		

Because the question items tap directly into competencies, they can also be used to yield a score on each of those. So, in addition to seeing if someone is altogether 'in the frame', the pattern of responses can be used to help the decision about who to hire. Look at the two sets of results in Table 6.2. Both of them come to the same total of 18 and both are quite well above the cut-off point of 15 as used in the example in Figure 6.1.However, candidate B is likely be more of a challenge to manage because of the variability in their scores. Also, they are not likely to be very good with people. The employer may be prepared to take candidate A if they think that people skills are in short supply in their team and they themselves might make up for the deficiency in results focus, or help A manage around that, perhaps by regular reviews of progress with them. The value to you as a candidate in knowing this is not to suggest that you should try to present yourself as less or as more extreme than you are, but to help you to understand that the employer applying this technique may gain valuable information that can be used in managing you after you are appointed. This can, of course, be done in principle with any psychometric measure, but it is more apparent with the SPI because it is designed directly around the competencies for the role.

Training of interview assessors

The use of these interviews hinges upon fine distinctions between right and wrong answers, that is fitting or not fitting the guidelines. To make these fine distinctions those assessing the results will have been through quite intense training. They will typically work with scripts of interviews from high and average performers based on the research and will be required to demonstrate that their

> in some cases the interviews will be recorded and transcribed

coding is strictly in agreement with the guidelines. They will also be trained in delivering the interviews, among other things sticking strictly to the wording as laid down.

In some cases the interviews will be recorded and transcribed and the assessor will work from the transcript. Thus interviewer and assessor are not necessarily one and the same person. More commonly interviewer and assessor will be the same and quite often that person will work with notes made at the same time as the interview rather than from a script.

What to do and what not to do

 **tip**

It is important to stick to the question and to give examples where asked for.

The guidance on what to do in response to these questions is similar to that provided in Chapter 4 on receiving feedback. As well as people just straying from the point some candidates rephrase the question and then answer their own version. If you do that you reduce your chances of hitting the guideline for the proper question.

You may think it goes without saying that an example describes a time when you did something, not a generality and not usually a claim that you do something 'all the time'. However, it is very common for candidates to become confused here and to talk about principles and approach when what has been asked for has been something very specific and concrete. In other words, you need to recreate the situation for the interviewer.

The interviewer should be prepared to repeat a question for you or allow you to come back to it at the end of the interview. What they will not do is to interpret the question for you: that is down to you, as it would be in a personality questionnaire. There may indeed be a degree of ambiguity, but that is how the approach works, particularly with those questions that deal with attitudes rather than ask for examples.

For some of the questions the guideline might call for a particular term to be known and understood, because the higher performers certainly do understand it, while the average performers do not. If you don't you will not receive credit and so there is no point in the interviewer explaining it to you. That would be rather like handing you the scoring key for an ability test. Take, for example, the question, 'Have you ever been told that you are empathetic?' Someone who is empathetic – attuned to the feelings of others – will have had the experience of being told that and will have got to know the word. Someone who is not empathetic will be less likely to have come across the term. (With this particular question, if a positive response is received a supplementary question would ask for a specific example. Only if this can be supplied will the response be given credit.)

Try to give a definite answer. If you are vague in your response or reply in terms of 'it all depends', the interviewer will not have a clear position to go from. In such a case even if your answer does cover the guideline, your commitment to it may not seem very firm. The interviewer will have been trained to look for definite responses and will have been told not to give the benefit of the doubt.

As we have seen, the interviewer will be listening for responses that fit the guidelines. Once those have been either been hit or totally negated in a response the interviewer will be ready to move on. They will probably signal that to you by saying 'OK' or 'thank you' and will not really make use of anything that you might say after that point. So listen out for these cues and the whole process will move ahead more quickly than if you keep elaborating and expanding on your response.

Using the sample material

Interviewers using the SPI approach may well feel uncomfortable with it at first. They think that it is somewhat restrictive and means that they cannot follow-up on responses that seem to them to need further investigation. Some believe that it can't possibly work, regardless of the research that says otherwise. This attitude is usually dispelled once they get to practise the technique, as opposed to being lectured about it or seeing the questions and guidelines written down.

brilliant tip

Because you are reading this from a book you may find that the technique does not come alive for you in the same way as the written tests do. Therefore you might like to try getting a friend to read the various sample questions to you to see how you find making the responses.

If you do follow the last Brilliant Tip you will probably notice several things. First, if you don't really have a relevant example to quote you will probably struggle to come up with one, even in a try-out situation. Under the pressure of a real interview this is likely to be more difficult. Second, when the question taps into familiar ground and something with which you are highly engaged, you will probably find it very easy to come up with relevant examples.

This issue of ease or difficulty in finding the right answer is important to understand in connection with a commonly-raised concern with this technique. That is, that people will tell you the answer you want to hear. If this were so then the technique just would not work. In turn that emphasises the importance of undertaking the careful research to develop these interviews. Along the way a large number of questions will have been tried out on high and average performers. Only those questions that actually distinguish between the two groups will have been retained. Thus the questions remaining in the interview are the ones that actually do distinguish between the higher and average performers – the ones that the latter have not been able to 'see through'.

Other types of structured interview

A range of types

Other types of structured interview cover a very wide range. At one end there are those where the only difference from the SPI is in the amount of research to back them. Thus questions will be arranged in runs and responses interpreted according to guidelines. Binary (1 or 0) coding might also be used. The design of the questions will be based on the views of the designers, typically working together with the organisation concerned. Hence there will be a rationale and system behind the process. However, given that there is no research base to establish the fine differences between high and lower performers, the training of the interviewers will usually be far less intense. Also, because it is difficult to distinguish what a high performer might give as an example to a hypothetical question from one provided by the average performer there will be even more emphasis on what has been done in the past. If anything, it makes it more important for you to

respond with examples when asked, rather than giving a hypothetical answer

respond with examples when asked, rather than giving a hypothetical answer or answering with something that might have been gleaned from a management textbook. In fact, you may not know if you have experienced an SPI or not. So the various points of guidance for responding to the SPI apply here, too.

There are other interviews which are more loosely structured. These arose in something like their present form as part of the assessment centre movement, which is discussed further in the next chapter. They used to be called 'criterion based interviews'. Today, they are more commonly known as 'competency-based interviews' though, technically, as seen this could also apply to the SPI.

In these interviews there is usually a core of common questions, but considerable scope is given for follow-up and probing by the interviewer. They veer towards the psychometric idea to the extent that there are some common questions and also due to the fact that the interviewers may produce ratings on a numerical scale. However these will not be binary ratings and will be less likely to have been arrived at by consideration of strict guidelines such as are applied to the SPI. Indeed, these interviews are included here essentially because they round out the picture on structured interviews. They are rather on the fringe of methods that can be considered to be psychometric and may not feel much different from a more conventional interview, which will tend to focus a lot on career history.

In this type of interview, though, there may be considerable rigour in the way follow-up questions are asked, particularly if the interviewers have been trained. It is worth noting this as you think about how you handle the questions. They will tend very much towards establishing just what you have done: you are unlikely to be asked about your philosophy of management at every turn, so avoid talking about it unless you actually are! The following types of questions are likely:

● What did you actually do?

brilliant tip

Be careful here about talking in terms of what 'we' did. The interviewer is interested in your own contribution and the impression here could be that you were just tagging along. You may be prompted to explain further whether you are using 'we' in talking about a team activity that you led, which may give you a chance to clarify what your own role was, which is obviously helpful to you if it was a significant one. However, often you will not be asked the follow-up, so by talking about 'we' you will have diluted the strength of your response.

● When did you do that?

brilliant tip

Recent examples tend to be regarded as better than ancient ones. There is a certain logic in that, although it is not perfect. For example, if you were asked about when you last praised someone and you give an example from five years ago, you will not convince that you are in the habit of delivering praise. On the other hand, if you are asked to indicate a major hurdle that you have overcome at work, an example going back a few years won't hurt.

- Who initiated that?

brilliant tip

Here the interviewer is probably trying to find out if you were the one with the bright idea and the sense of purpose to set things in motion. So it is better to choose examples where you have been the prime mover if you can. If you were not, then it is better to say so directly rather than to give a rambling account of why 'it didn't work like that'.

- Why did you do that?

brilliant tip

This question may be exploring your motives and therefore your tendency to behave in a particular way, so answers like, 'I realised there was a risk if we didn't cover that' will be looked for. In other cases the question is aimed at establishing, again, how much scope you really had to do things. So if your response is, 'Because I was told to', it won't carry a great deal of weight. Again, think about your examples.

- How large was that piece of work?

brilliant tip

There may be a variety of questions of this sort, all aimed at finding out about the scope and extent of what you have been doing. If the job you are going for has responsibilities over large numbers of people and resources then it will be as well to pick out an example that reflects similar responsibilities from your own background.

- What was the result?

 **tip**

Here the interviewer will be looking for a focus on outcomes and a capacity to deliver. You may need to be careful about examples you choose. So if you were getting on pretty well with a piece of work, but it was cancelled before you actually got to the end of it, that will make a less convincing story than something taken to a conclusion. The same applies if you left prior to a particular project being finished.

- How did you do that?

 **tip**

Some organisations emphasise how things were done as well as the result. What they are looking for are some of the main elements of your approach, not the recollections from your mental diary of a year-long project. This can be a real danger if you lived and breathed a major piece of work that you found absorbing and challenging. The fine details are unlikely to be of interest or, indeed, of use to the interviewer. What they will be after will be some of the main strands in what went on: did you make an overall plan? Did you recognise who needed to be brought on-side? Did you arrange for any special activities such as training for yourself or others so as to get the job done?

Why not answer the question?

Again, the rule 'do answer the question' applies here and that extends to not challenging the question. Remember that when interviews are structured the questions are being asked for a reason. Some of the types of responses that won't gain you much credit are illustrated in the following Brilliant Example. All of them are real and recent.

brilliant example

The following are examples of bad answers:

Question   What would you do if you were given a blank sheet in this job?

Bad answer   I don't think you would be given that.

The candidate is in effect telling the interviewer that they are a fool for asking the question, which was probably intended to explore the ability to 'think outside the box'. The candidate has shown that they probably don't think like that.

Question   You have indicated your ideas for using modern marketing methods in connection with the services of the college. What are the arguments against that approach?

Bad answer   I think you really have to go with the modern methods.

The interviewer already knows that is what the candidate thinks. They were exploring whether they could put themselves in the shoes of another person and so have more chance of persuading them.

Question   What did you find the biggest obstacle in delivering that piece of work?

Bad answer   Well, you always get obstacles in any project; you just have to learn to cope.

The interviewer knows that and the question implies it. Had the candidate identified a specific obstacle that would probably have provoked a follow-up about how it was overcome. As it is the interviewer might well make a note saying 'overoptimistic?'

Mixing and matching

These types of interview questions may also be used together with other approaches, such as presentations. In these cases they are likely to follow on from questions particularly related to the points made in the presentation, but may then take on something of a life of their own. Some candidates find this rather a surprise and, hence, quite demanding. So, if you are asked to prepare a presentation and told that there will be a period of questioning afterwards, be alert to the fact that it is likely to use the competency-based approach and to move away to some extent from just probing your presentation.

There are yet other types of structured interviews in which you will be given one or more scenarios in some detail and asked to describe how you would deal with them. These are called 'situational' interviews. The interviewer will probe, probably challenging you on various points and introducing changes or further developments in the scenario. This probably takes us further still from the psychometric field, but there will still be particular things that the interviewer is seeking. That is, they will still be assessing you in terms of competencies. If you study the Brilliant Action opposite describing a situational interview item you will see that it is similar to the SPI hypothetical question illustrated in Table 6.1. However, it is a bit more detailed and the probing is likely to be more wide-ranging. Indeed, there may be no probing in the SPI case.

 **action**

Situational interview item

Suppose that you have been working on a piece of work with a junior colleague and it now needs to be written up as a report. She has done well so far and your boss suggests to you that it would be a good developmental experience for her to take the lead in the write-up. From what you have seen of her written work it is satisfactory, but not outstanding. When you put your boss's suggestion to her she says that she doesn't really like writing and would rather not take the lead as suggested. What would you do?

I have made the point that in their various forms structured interviews are more or less psychometric. Whatever their precise form they are all relatively systematised methods of enquiry, so they are not just cosy chats in which the questions are meant to stimulate you to ramble on or to keep repeating how great you are. There is no substitute for listening to the questions and answering them.

CHAPTER 7

Other 'tests'

A range of approaches

There are a number of other means of assessment that follow psychometric principles to a greater or lesser extent. Of these the largest category is provided by assessment centres, which may often include the more regular psychometrics amongst the procedures used. However these will be ranged alongside a variety of other processes as described later in this chapter. The first two types of 'test' referred to here differ from other psychometrics in the positioning of the candidate in relation to the employer. In the first, the self-screener, it is typically the candidate who decides on the basis of the results whether or not to pursue an application for a job. In the second, 360° assessments, development rather than selection is usually the aim. In both of these, psychometric principles may be more strictly applied than with the other forms of 'test' described in this chapter.

Self-screeners

With a self-screener you are presented with a questionnaire in a format similar to that used in a personality measure and with questions that again tap into typical performance. However, rather than producing a readout on a number of dimensions you will be given a single score and advised as to whether or not it is worthwhile continuing with your application. As with screening using the SPI approach as discussed in the last chapter, or the

you will be given a
single score and advised
as to whether or not it is
worthwhile continuing

Verify method referred to in Chapter 5, the idea is that a preliminary assessment may save time being wasted later on candidates with little chance of success. The difference with those methods is that, with self-screening, the decision as to whether to be guided by the result lies with you, the candidate. Your results will probably be presented to you in one of three categories:

1   you have little chance of making it through the selection process proper;
2   you have a reasonable chance or;
3   you have quite a good chance.

If your results fall into the last category you might also be advised to consider if you have asked the questions absolutely honestly. (There is, perhaps, even less sense in answering other than honestly with a self-screening instrument than with any other personality or motivation questionnaire: it is only yourself you are kidding.)

Note that the result will have been presented with a relatively crude indication, based on a total score rather than one looking at nuances amongst different scales. So you might feel that, regardless of an indication to the contrary, you do have what it takes to succeed in the job. Perhaps you are looking at a sales job and are convinced that you are very persuasive. If so, then you might decide to invest time and effort in a full application. Sometimes you will succeed, but the odds will definitely be against you.

The self-screening approach is particularly popular with organisations that are household names and particularly if the job has a superficially glamorous appeal. One such system was used by an organisation that was an international bank, instantly recog-

nisable to all and the job was that of international banking offi-
cer. So there were the attractions of a famous and worthy brand
and international travel. What was not so apparent was that the
international travel might involve uprooting oneself at a
moment's notice and moving for an indeterminate period, possibly several years, to a part of the world that might provide a
pleasant and stimulating environment or one that could be
decidedly hostile.

The self-screening questionnaire sought to explore candidates'
fit to these circumstances, with questions looking at degree of
dependency on family and friends, interest in other cultures
and attitudes to diet, among other things. The bank found that
the number of applications dropped by half and that the proportion of those considered appointable rose substantially. This
obviously saved them considerable effort in 'processing'
unpromising candidates and also reduced the number of people
being disappointed after spending time on a full application.

In a variation of the self-screening process you receive the
results in the normal way, but the employing organisation also
gets to see them, so can decide whether or not to take your
application further and can also use the screening results
directly at the next stage. It will generally be made clear to you
whether or not this is being done.

360° assessments

In a 360° assessment you are asked to rate yourself on a number
of dimensions and your colleagues are asked to rate you, too.
Colleagues will typically be those at the same level – your peers –
together with your boss and your subordinates, if any. Thus the
approach is only fully applicable if you have responsibility for
managing or supervising others. Also, it obviously only works for
those already in a job, so it is not applicable to selection. It is

used rather for performance management and may be linked in with an appraisal process. (Some organisations pay bonuses to managers based on the ratings of those they manage.)

The results of the 360° will be presented to you in terms of your ratings – the self-ratings and those of the other respondents. Differences between these two sets will often be discussed with you in a feedback session, which might be with your manager or with a third party. The ratings of the other respondents will typically be averaged, but you might also be shown the range of ratings given, that is the highest score you were awarded and the lowest. The results will be anonymised, which encourages the other people to be truthful in their responses.

The questions may be from published sources and standardised with results reported in terms of fixed competencies. (There is one such published questionnaire that uses seven competencies and I have just completed the design of another with five.) Alternatively the questions may be designed on a bespoke basis for a particular application in a particular organisation. The standardised approach comes much closer to a psychometric model given that norms are available. Very often, particularly with bespoke 360° approaches, the other respondents will also have the opportunity to add comments. These will again be reported to you anonymously. They may be completely free-format or they may be under headings such as 'stop doing', 'start doing' and 'continue doing'.

> the only real guidance is, as ever, to be honest

So are there any things that you should think about if asked to undertake a 360° process? The only real guidance is, as ever, to be honest. The added twist to this is that if you are not, this is likely to show itself in major discrepancies between your ratings and those of your colleagues. Hence the 'faking good' involved will be if anything more apparent than the response style indicators in a personality measure (see Chapter 4).

Also, think about how to handle the feedback that you will get; it may be some of the most powerful information that you ever receive about yourself. Sometimes people's response to negative ratings or comments about themselves has been to try to work out who has supplied that rating or made that comment. This can descend into a witch hunt, with a clear intention to punish. Clearly, if this line is pursued it is likely to lead to negative outcomes, perhaps the least of which is to lessen the chances of the 360° process being applied effectively (if at all) in that organisation or department in the future.

You may find that your ratings are on the whole lower than those of your colleagues. If this is the case it may reflect a general modesty on your part which, taken to an extreme, could amount to a severe lack of self-esteem. Alternatively, it might reflect the fact that some at least of your colleagues – maybe peers in particular if you don't work closely with them – don't actually know you very well.

If you find that your ratings are generally higher than those of your colleagues, then you may have an inflated view of yourself. This is worth thinking about. The temptation will be to deny the indications, but this could mean that you are sleepwalking to disaster! More commonly you may find that there is substantial agreement between the self-ratings and those of others, but one or two marked differences. This is where examination of the comments, when available, can be particularly helpful, as they may give you clues to negative aspects of your behaviour of which you have been unaware yourself and about which colleagues have been reluctant to inform you. With all of this there will be value in considering the results together with any other feedback that you have had about yourself, perhaps from an appraisal, so as to refine your self-insights further.

Assessment centres – bits of the job under the microscope

What to expect

If you are asked to attend an assessment centre you can expect to complete a number of activities, which might well include personality and ability psychometrics and structured interviews. You will also be likely to be given one or more of a number of exercises, such as in-baskets, role-plays or written analysis exercises. You are quite likely, too, to find yourself in a group discussion exercise together with other candidates. Typical of all of these exercises is that they aim to create a fairly accurate reproduction of part of the role concerned. In fact, they are often referred to as 'job simulation exercises'.

There is actually a rather strict definition of what constitutes an assessment centre (see the Brilliant Definition below), though in practice the term is often applied more loosely to any place in which a number of assessment activities are involved. However, they will always include more than one assessment method and typically at least one will be a job simulation exercise of the type referred to above and described in more detail below.

 brilliant definition

The defining characteristics of assessment centres are as follows:

Job analysis
This is conducted in advance of attendance at the centre to decide what is to be assessed. Different methods can be used, including focus groups and one-to-one discussions with 'subject matter experts', i.e. people who know about the job.

Multiple exercises
A detailed picture is built up by giving candidates the opportunity to perform in a number of different situations.

Multiple assessors
Several different people take part in the assessment process, helping to iron out biases and to achieve consistency.

Assessor training
Assessors are trained in the principles and practices of assessment and familiarised with the specific exercises to be used.

Stepwise process
The job simulation exercises are assessed by a stepwise process of observe, record, classify, evaluate – known as the ORCE model.

Assessor panel discussion
Sometimes called the wash-up discussion, this is where the assessors discuss their findings and agree on their ratings.

The assessment centre will be arranged to allow coverage of several competencies by each assessment method used and to give a minimum of two opportunities for each competency to be tested. Some assessment methods, whether 'standard' test, interview or job simulation exercise, will be seen as particularly strong sources of information. These points are illustrated in Table 7.1.

Table 7.1 Competencies by exercises

Competency	In-tray	Role-play	Group discussion	Numerical reasoning
Strategic thinking	✓✓		✓	
Commercial awareness	✓	✓		✓
Planning & organising	✓✓	✓	✓	
Communications	✓	✓✓	✓✓	
Interpersonal		✓✓	✓✓	
Delegation	✓✓	✓		
Performance management	✓	✓✓		✓

✓ = standard source
✓✓ = strong source

Because of the multiple coverage of the competencies, if you have done poorly in one you have the opportunity to redeem yourself in others. By the same token the total picture built up by the assessment centre, with its scope for cross-checking of indications across the different assessment methods used, is likely to be quite compelling to the recruiting organisation and so be less likely to be set aside than the results of a single or a couple of standard psychometrics alone. The type of evidence that can emerge is shown in Table 7.2, showing the ratings for a single candidate, where 1 is low and 5 is high. As you can see this person appears to have done well in the individual exercises, but less so in those that required interaction with others, giving a further slant on dealings with people beyond that provided by the ratings on each competency. In arriving at these ratings the assessors will have followed a detailed assessment guide indicating how each competency can be expected to be demonstrated in each exercise and how they should be evaluated.

In some exercises you will be asked to complete a participant report form at the end (see the Brilliant Example opposite). This will provide supplementary information to that given in the exercise itself and will be studied by the assessing team.

Table 7.2 Assessment centre ratings

Competency	In-tray	Role-play	Group discussion	Numerical reasoning
Strategic thinking	3		2	
Commercial awareness	4	3		5
Planning & organising	3	3	2	
Communications	3	2	2	
Interpersonal		2	2	
Delegation	3	2		
Performance management	4	3		5

Some candidates write at great length on these forms, but it is worth noting that they are not meant to give an opportunity for some sort of re-run of the exercise, but rather as a chance to make some marginal comments. These comments may affect the ratings given, but not by much.

 **example**

Participant report form questions

Group discussion

1   How did you approach the exercise?

2   If you were to do it again, would you approach it differently?

3   Did anything prevent you from doing as well as you could have done?

4   What was agreed in the meeting?

5   What role did you play in the meeting?

6   Can you identify roles played by any others in the meeting?

You are rather less likely with job simulation exercises than with the standard psychometrics to be given sample material in advance, although you might be given some hints and tips on the approach to take. However, this will probably be the exception rather than the rule and where they are given such suggestions may be quite sketchy. Given that fact and the compelling nature of the findings as noted above, you might like to pay particular attention to the various points to watch out for in the different types of exercise described below. These are essentially mistakes to avoid rather than guaranteed recipes for success.

Group discussions

Group discussions typically involve a number of candidates being required to work together on a task or series of tasks. Occasionally candidates are taken aback by this requirement, particularly if they personally know or know about some of the others in the running. Although less common for very senior posts than for others, group discussions are sometimes used here, too, and are run for positions up to chief executives of local authorities and major charities. If it is not clear from what you have been told about the assessment centre in advance that you will experience such an exercise, and if you have some concerns about meeting colleagues in such a forum, then do at least ask. The designers of the assessment centre may feel that the group discussion is so much their stock-in-trade that it will not necessarily occur to them to give a specific warning.

There are various types of group discussion, with the principal ones being non-assigned and assigned role and there is also a hybrid semi-assigned role type. There is usually a period of individual preparation in advance of the discussion itself. The discussion will be observed by a number of assessors, who will typically concentrate on observing and recording what is said and done by two candidates, although they will also make some notes on the whole of the proceedings. The participant report form may ask you to comment on the role that you felt you played in the meeting and to identify roles played by others, as in the Brilliant Example on the previous page. This is not to get you to function as an assessor but, rather, to see if you show awareness of the contribution that you made. Thus, if you saw yourself as leading the meeting, but this was not identified by the assessors, it could constitute some negative evidence in terms of self-insight.

Non-assigned role

In a non-assigned role group discussion, candidates are asked to work together on a single topic or series of topics. The single topic might range from a social issue in the public domain, such as the legalisation of soft drugs or be built around a case study, such as a problem with an IT system used for procurement. In either case the group would be required to discuss the topic so as to come up with a conclusion or a way forward. Series of topics are often of the 'management problems' variety, such as issues in a manufacturing plant arising from a merger with another facility.

The relatively unstructured nature of the task means that candidates need to work out their approach to the meeting as well as addressing the problem(s) set. How they do this will provide evidence in areas including planning and organising or influence.

Assigned role

In this type of exercise, each candidate is given a part to play, typically with a strong element of advocacy involved. Examples include evaluating entries in a company suggestion scheme, where each candidate would be required to speak on behalf of a different short-listed entry, or deciding between different firms bidding for accommodation on a university science park. The different alternatives are designed so that there are pros and cons in each case, rather than a natural winner, giving a basis for discussion. Although more structured than the non-assigned role discussion, with a pretty clear indication that each case needs to be heard, there is still a need for candidates to work out the approach that they will take.

Semi-assigned role

This is a term that I have coined for those exercises which are midway between the assigned and non-assigned type. Typically there are a number of positions or issues to consider and each candidate is instructed to lead on one of them. Everybody has outline information on all of the issues, but detail on only one of them. Thus there is a need for each position or issue to be explained and scope for follow-up questioning by other candidates. The fact that each candidate has something on which to lead largely guarantees some participation by all, but emphasis is placed on sharing information and coming to agreement, thereby diluting the advocacy aspect. Sometimes there will be issues available for discussion but without a lead person having been assigned and note will be taken of whether or not these are dealt with. This will be a part of looking at the approach taken.

Points to watch in the group discussion – some general and some specific to the different types – are given in the Brilliant Tips below.

brilliant tips

When taking part in a group discussion, remember the following:

- It may seem obvious, but don't try to talk all of the time.
- Again, obvious, but do talk some of the time, otherwise the assessors will have no information to go on.
- Consider your posture in the meeting; don't shut others out by turning your back on them for instance.
- In an assigned role discussion, make your case but don't insist on your position at all costs. Remember that you will be assessed on a number of things, not just your forcefulness.
- Don't talk to the observing assessors: they are not participants and have been briefed not to take part.
- Don't use the participant report form as a chance to excuse yourself if you think you have done badly.

- Watch the time and don't rely on others even if someone else has volunteered to be the timekeeper. In many group discussions the participants mistake the time left to them by several minutes.

- If you are the one who volunteers or agrees to be timekeeper, make sure that you do it properly. If you don't you may be marked down on attention to detail.

- Similarly, if it is agreed that you are chairing the meeting, make sure that you do so, for example ensuring all have a chance to speak, summarising and confirming agreements. Speak up so that you can be heard by the assessors as well as the other participants. Oral communication may be assessed. Also, if they cannot hear you properly the assessors may not grasp your ideas.

- Don't ask the other participants what you are supposed to be doing. If you don't understand the initial brief ask the administrator.

- Don't try to start the discussion or to chat to the other participants during the period of individual preparation.

- Don't ask for more time to study the brief. If you ask this of the administrator it will not be granted. If you ask your fellow candidates and they agree, no behaviour will be noted during that extra period beyond yours of delaying the proceedings.

- Don't interrupt other people unless they seem to be going on far too long.

- Don't allow yourself to be interrupted and if someone else attempts to do so politely ask to finish your point.

- Be clear about what, if anything, has been agreed. Follow the discussion and comment at the time if you don't agree.

- Be careful about being the scribe for the group. You may find yourself just taking dictation from a pushier participant. If you are the scribe be active, for instance summarising points and reading out what you have down.

▶

- Don't be too eager to leap up and write on a flip-chart. You might establish a position of leadership by doing so, but you might find yourself isolated from the discussion and, again, possibly just taking dictation.

- Don't jump into the detail of your own views on the topic to be discussed. This is particularly a temptation in the assigned role discussion, but even there the group will need to work out how it is to operate.

In-basket exercises

In an in-basket exercise you will find yourself presented with items of correspondence to handle, representing those typically dealt with by someone in the type of role for which you are applying. The fit to the real-life items may be very close, having been taken from actual correspondence dealt with by the out-going incumbent of the role, with little modification beyond making the material anonymous. In other cases an off-the-shelf exercise will be used, representing the type of correspondence likely to be encountered at the level of the target job and in the sector concerned. In either case you are depicted as being due to take over the role from a predecessor in a few weeks' time, but being prevented from receiving a smooth handover by that person having been taken ill or being in an accident.

You are portrayed as having agreed to come into the office to handle the items that have built up in the unfortunate person's in-basket. The time for you to do that is usually set at the week-end, with no other people about and no direct access to e-mail or telephone. You will also be told that you only have a limited time to handle the correspondence – one to two hours is common – before leaving the country for an important personal or business engagement overseas. You will be asked to leave instructions for your assistant to progress the material as you see fit, as well as to indicate plans for any future meetings. The overseas trip will last for a couple of weeks and you will take up your role properly on your return. Because of your travel schedule you will not be able to make contact with your new organisation until you get back.

All of this is to tell you that you just have the allotted time to work with the material presented and no recourse to information other than that given to you. This information will usually include some background on the organisation concerned as well as the items of correspondence. You may be told that you can make any other assumptions that might seem reasonable to you, for example on the existence of particular bodies or posts in the organisation depicted, but you will be asked to make such assumptions clear.

The items of correspondence are likely to include a mix of short-term operational matters and those of a policy or strategic nature. There will often be themes running through a number of items and there may be some explicit links. For example, there could be evidence of different departments not talking to one another or a tendency to pass matters upwards for resolution.

Usually you will be asked to complete a participant report form after an in-basket. This will provide additional data, particularly about any themes that you have seen in the correspondence or the groups and individuals with whom you would particularly wish to establish working relationships. Less commonly you might be asked to undergo an in-basket interview. This will be performed by an assessor after a preliminary review of your work. They will explore the reasons for some of the actions taken or not taken – did you leave a particular item because you saw it as unimportant or because you ran out of time? As well, they will probe your understanding of the links amongst various items.

brilliant tips

When dealing with in-baskets, remember the following:

- Look at the urgency and the importance of each item.
- Consider if there is a 'political' dimension to an item, e.g. interest by a member of parliament or the press.
- If you decide to delegate something, think about whether you need to express your own intentions.
- Use the participant report form carefully; assessors will be looking for insights you have gained, rather than excuses or criticisms.
- Keep an eye on the time; you won't necessarily be expected to respond to all of the items, but if you only address half of them there will:
  a. not be much to go on and
  b. a question mark over your time management.
- Consider the audience to whom you are writing and be careful with technical terms and particularly abbreviations.
- Look for links amongst items.
- The approach of just dealing with the items one after another means that you may pay insufficient attention to important ones that occur late on in the in-basket.
- You will usually be expected to frame responses rather than just indicating how you would respond.
- If you leave a secretary or PA to formulate the detail of a response on a sensitive 'political' personal issue, you will not be demonstrating much sensitivity yourself.
- Be careful not to mix up the characters depicted; passing something to your boss that should go to a subordinate will be viewed negatively!

- Respond in role; if you are told that you are Jo(e) Bloggs for the purpose of the exercise then use that name.
- Be alert for issues with diversity implications; some of these might be hidden. For example, if someone suggests a series of breakfast meetings will it occur to you to consider how the early start to the day might affect those of your staff with childcare or other caring responsibilities?
- Make an effort. If you only work on half the items, there will be relatively little to go on and the fact that you haven't done much will be seen negatively.
- Be alert to confidentiality issues. For example, if someone has written to you to complain about their boss, think about if and how you will involve the boss.

Role-plays

In a role-play exercise you will be asked to play a part and a role-player will take a part opposite you. You will usually be given briefing material on the situation depicted and time to prepare. The situation, in terms of the background to the 'story', may quite closely reflect something likely to be encountered in the job concerned. Alternatively, it might be set in a different situation as far as specifics are concerned, but still reflect the real-life requirements in terms of the types of issues and challenges faced. These might include a performance management meeting with a staff member, a briefing meeting with a superior or an interaction with a client – internal or external. In each case there is likely to be a problem presented and then further information that might emerge in the course of the meeting, depending partly on the skill of the candidate. In the Brilliant Example shown overleaf, the second candidate picks up and pursues the cue about personal problems, while the first fails to do so.

 **brilliant** example

Role-play exercise passage

Candidate A (as boss)	So how did you get on with ensuring the co-operation of the stakeholders?
Subordinate	Well, the people from the XYZ Agency and the community groups were fine, but it has been more difficult to get hold of everyone in the regional set-up. Quite frankly they aren't inclined to be co-operative and it isn't helped by the fact that they are, of course, so spread out and my own personal situation does make for some difficulties.
Candidate A	So how confident are you that you will have cracked it by the end of next month, as per the original schedule?
Candidate B (as boss)	So how did you get on with ensuring the co-operation of the stakeholders?
Subordinate	Well, the people from the XYZ Agency and the community groups were fine, but it has been more difficult to get hold of everyone in the regional set-up. Quite frankly they aren't inclined to be co-operative and it isn't helped by the fact that they are, of course, so spread out and my own personal situation does make for some difficulties.
Candidate B	Your personal situation; I don't think I know about that, can you tell me more?

Refer again to Table 7.1 and you will see that such an exercise can be designed to yield information in quite a number of competencies. Whether or not the cues such as that shown in the Brilliant Example were picked up would, for instance, provide evidence of interpersonal skills. Evidence on commercial awareness could be given by the candidate raising questions about budgets or sales records and on planning and organising by plans for future activities actually being spelt out. Hence it would not be a matter of just going in and focusing on the immediate performance aspects of the situation, although these would need to be addressed. The brief to the superior might involve recommendations about which of a number of courses of action to pursue. The role-player would usually have been supplied with a number of arguments against each of the different possibilities – providing scope, for example, for the candidate's persuasiveness to be assessed.

Supplementary information can again be given by a participant report form, which might include a question about what was agreed by the two parties. Also, the assessor will often debrief the role-player, for example asking about behaviour that made a negative or positive impact.

brilliant tips

- Be on the lookout for both short- and long-term aspects of the situation depicted.
- Expect there to be more information available than that given directly in the brief and be prepared to explore that with the role-player. Be alert to hints of these in the brief (e.g. 'some problems were experienced with . . .'), or from the role-player (e.g. 'I have had one or two issues with my team . . .').
- Note that there will almost always be both people and operational aspects to contend with.
- Stay in role.
- Ignore the observer.

- Use your preparation time to make a plan for the meeting and try to stick to it, without being rigid.

- Listen, don't just tell.

- Ask for opinions.

- Try to agree some next steps.

- Recognise that there may be limits to the knowledge of the role-player and don't push them on technical points as you are likely just to be stonewalled.

Written analyses

Case studies

The most common type of written exercise is the case study. You are presented with a topic of some complexity to analyse and asked to prepare a report indicating your understanding of the situation and (usually) making recommendations for the way ahead. The topic might be something very closely related to the role, where you would be expected to bring a degree of specialist knowledge to bear. Alternatively, it might be a subject more generally in the public domain, for example the change in licensing laws to allow 24-hour opening of pubs and bars. In either case you will be given a number of pieces of information, which might include facts and figures, expert opinion and the representations of interested parties. So, in the licensing case you might have police statistics on changes in arrests for drunk and disorderly behaviour, views of community groups and business reports from the licensed trade. Your first challenge will be to make sense of what you are presented with and then you will need to weigh up the pros and cons of different possibilities for action.

brilliant tips

- Watch the time; there is a danger of getting bogged down in detail and not finishing the task.
- Be alert to long-term as well as short-term issues.
- Avoid copying out the information presented to you; it takes up time and doesn't demonstrate understanding.
- If you are presented with figures, do something with them.
- Don't be afraid to indicate that further information might be needed about some aspects of the situation depicted.
- If asked for plans or next steps make sure that you do indicate these.

Situational judgement tests

The term 'test' is applied to this form of assessment because it most closely resembles standard psychometrics. You are given a series of scenarios, each depicting a problem situation, and asked to indicate one of a number of alternative responses. The marking process evaluates these responses in terms of the ability to distinguish effective from ineffective responses.

In a variation on this approach, whilst you will again be presented with a number of alternative scenarios, you will not be presented with alternative answers. Instead you will be asked to indicate your understanding of the situation and come up with a way ahead. Thus this form of test is more in the tradition of the other job simulation exercises and, in particular, resembles the case study; each situation presented is in effect a mini case. The situational judgement approach can be seen as having something in common with the hypothetical questions that you will encounter in some of the situational interview questions covered in Chapter 6.

 action

Situational judgement test examples

- You have been working on an advertising campaign for a client for the last few months and everything is ready to be launched next week. You receive an e-mail from your routine contact in the client organisation saying that their new head of department wants to make some changes that will put the launch back by two weeks. They realise there will be some costs associated with the changes, but don't expect these to be much. You note that the delay will mean a clash with other work.

  What should be your next step?

  a. Find out what the changes actually are.

  b. Check the terms of the contract with the client.

  c. Call a meeting of your team to tell them about the delay.

  d. Try to reschedule the other work.

- A peer level colleague tells you that she has overheard some gossip about redundancies in the company and is worried about her job as she thinks the management is inclined to be unfair to women. What should you do?

  a. Tell her not to listen to gossip.

  b. Re-assure her that she won't be discriminated against.

  c. Tell her that if she is made redundant ahead of male colleagues she should raise a formal grievance.

  d. Express sympathy but take no action.

  e. Ask HR if there is any truth in the rumours.

Yet more assessment centre tools

Presentations

Presentations represent the most common activities included in assessment centres. You might sometimes be asked to make a presentation there, though more commonly this will be a part of a final panel. The scoring for a presentation is likely to be less formalised than for standard psychometrics or for any of the exercise types discussed above and this topic will not be explored further here. However, if you are anticipating making a presentation, either in connection with selection or otherwise, you might like to refer to Richard Hall's *Brilliant Presentation*, another volume in this series.

Fact-finding

Fact-finding exercises are less commonly used than the other types discussed in this chapter, so will not be covered in detail. As with case studies you are presented with background information and as with role-plays there is another party involved. However, that party is described as a 'resource person' rather than a role-player. They have further information which you can extract by questioning, after which you will be asked to make a decision and give reasons for it. You may then be given any further information that you have failed to uncover and asked if your initial decision still stands. The points to watch for in case studies and role-plays will be widely applicable if you do encounter a fact-finding exercise.

> the scoring for a presentation is likely to be less formalised than for standard psychometrics

So, there are many approaches that you may encounter, used alongside 'regular' psychometrics and sometimes incorporating them. They vary in the degree of rigour that they use, but they all represent systematic attempts to discover relevant information about you, the candidate.

CHAPTER 8

Testing fairly

Objectivity

The principle behind testing is to provide objective information on which to base decisions, such as who should be offered a job, and thereby optimise the fairness of the selection process. However, despite all the care and effort that goes into testing, there can be no absolute guarantee of fairness. This chapter explores some of the things that you can do to make sure you are being treated as fairly as possible and what to do if you think that you are not. Some of these points are matters of courtesy to you as a candidate, and of good professional standards in the use of tests, but some of them are backed by the force of law.

What you should be told

You can expect to be told the purpose of the test and how the results will be used. This information may be given in advance when you are invited to the testing session, or at the time of testing. If the test is actually to be used as a hurdle, that is, with a definite cut-off, then you should be told that it is to be used in that way. In fact the use of cut-offs is only really applicable to ability tests and usually then only in high-volume testing situations. In other cases you will probably be advised that the testing process is to provide information to a recruiting manager or a panel, but that other information will also be taken into account. If you ask just how the information is to be used the administrator is unlikely to be able to tell you much more as the recruiting manager or panel involved will not be applying a set formula to the use of the tests. That is not meant to put you off; it is rather a reflection of the fact that individuals and panels vary tremendously in the notice that they take of psychometric results.

Very often you will be provided with a job description and person specification for the job and the latter might well contain a list of competencies and characteristics. It is worth looking at this quite carefully as you think about what testing processes you are being asked to complete and, if necessary, mounting a challenge. You will probably not have the expertise to check out everything in this way, but there may be some things that really stand out. In one case a company was using a test of mechanical reasoning for a job that appeared to have no mechanical component. When queried they responded: 'We've got a cupboard full of them and management won't let us buy anything else until they are all used up.' More commonly you might find that you are being asked to take a numerical reasoning test for a job with no apparent numerical content. If so do query that; does the job have hidden components or is the test being used as a 'general' measure? Neither of these answers would hold water professionally.

> you should also be told if feedback is to be given and when

You should also be told if feedback is to be given and when. As discussed in Chapter 4 this will usually be done prior to a report on you being written and will be a two-way process, giving you some ideas about the strengths and limitations that you might display as well as exemplifying those to the person reporting on you. Although feedback at some stage is regarded as good practice, it is not made an absolute necessity in professional guidance for testing. Certainly there is no set way in which feedback is to be given and whether or not documentation, such as the printout of a personality questionnaire's results, is handed over will vary from situation to situation.

Examples and practice

As indicated in Chapter 2 you will often be given examples and the opportunity for practice with ability tests. For personality measures and job simulation exercises you will be given instructions on the day as well as some indication in advance of what is involved. You clearly have the right to know what you are supposed to be doing and there should be the opportunity for you to ask if anything is not clear.

As noted in Chapter 7, you might want to enquire if a group discussion is to be involved at an assessment centre. In general if you don't want to come into contact with other candidates you should say so. The employing organisation or the recruiters working on their behalf will usually respect this and make their arrangements accordingly. If you are attending a residential assessment event in particular, you might want to check if a dress code is required. Obviously it is more courteous for you to be told without asking, but you may save yourself embarrassment by enquiring if it is not made clear. I once attended a residential assessment centre where the administrator announced on the evening of arrival that the dress code was casual, which was a bit problematic for the candidates who had assumed that business dress would be appropriate.

brilliant tip

Consider whether you will have problems in coming into contact with other candidates and, if so, alert those responsible for the testing session in good time.

Discrimination

Direct and indirect

The law distinguishes between two types of discrimination: direct and indirect. In *direct discrimination*, membership of a particular group, for example in terms of gender, race or disability, is used as the criterion as to who to hire or not to hire; this is illegal. In the world of testing, the test itself could actually help prevent direct discrimination or help bring it to light if it had occurred. For example, if out of five candidates the one man scored far lower on a test than the four women, but was nevertheless hired, that would suggest that the decision on who to hire was being made on the basis of gender alone – a case of direct discrimination.

In *indirect discrimination*, the possession of characteristics related to a particular group, rather than membership of that group itself, is taken as the criterion for selection. Such discrimination is also illegal unless it can be demonstrated by the employer that the characteristics chosen are essential for the job. For example, to rule out men who sometimes wear the kilt as part of the selection process would be to discriminate against Scotsmen and illegally so, as this tendency would be unlikely to have relevance for the jobs in question.

Tests have sometimes been implicated in indirect discrimination. There was a case some years ago in which a group of Asian applicants to a factory sued the employer successfully, having failed to be appointed after taking a reading comprehension test. The employer argued that they needed to demonstrate that they could understand safety notices. However, the vocabulary used and the cut-offs applied were far beyond those required for this task and the candidates did not have English as their mother tongue. Had the test used language more in keeping with that actually used in the safety notices, then the relevance of the test would probably have been upheld, and many of the Asian candidates would probably have passed it, too.

Special needs

Indirect discrimination can arise with candidates who have special needs but with good test practice there will be opportunities for you to indicate such needs and so avoid indirect discrimination. Someone with poor eyesight may be discriminated against if required to take a test using print size for those with average or better eyesight. A person with hearing difficulties may be discriminated against in a group discussion if they are unable to hear clearly what others are saying. In such cases it is worth pointing out that in dealing with those who are disabled, there is a requirement for the employer to

> indirect discrimination can arise with candidates who have special needs

consider if the person could do the job with reasonable adjustment. For example, for those with speech difficulties, consideration might be given to providing them with software to translate typed messages into audio format, enabling them to participate in teleconferences.

Thus there is the question of adjustment at two levels: in testing and on the job. If you do have special needs it will help you to make sure that all those involved in the process of decision-making about the job are alert to your disability. As far as testing goes you will typically be asked as part of your initial invitation to undertake tests to flag such needs. Indeed, those responsible for testing may even be aware of this in advance, for instance if the testing is set up as the second or later stage of a recruitment process.

Once alerted, those responsible for the testing will usually contact you to discuss just how you might be helped. If you are partially sighted or blind and usually dictate your correspondence then, if asked to take, say, a written analysis test, you might be provided with someone to read the material to you and type your dictated responses. There are also Braille versions of some tests, but these may take a few days for the testing team to acquire. If you are dyslexic you may well have certification to advise potential employers as to how the time for tests should be extended for you.

It is worth noting, though, that the tests are generally designed for those without special needs and this has some implications. First, it may not be possible to make any suitable adjustment to some tests or exercise. For example, for someone who is totally deaf, it would be difficult to set up a group discussion that would work. Processes such as one-to-one lip reading or signing would be impracticable in such circumstances. If there is such an area for you then those concerned might consider setting up a different situation for you, basing that for instance on your indicating how you do normally manage to communicate with others.

Another implication is that those responsible for testing need to keep in mind that they have to be as fair as possible to all candidates, not just those who are disabled, and that there is no foolproof formula for this. Thus, if as a dyslexic person you are given half as long again as other candidates to complete a verbal ability test, that might be seen as OK by other candidates, but should you be given three times as long or would that give you an unfair advantage? The test users have to weigh up all of this and try to come to a resolution, but this will often involve a degree of compromise by all parties.

It is worth noting here that those involved in testing often put considerable effort into accommodating people with special needs. For example, a number of test publishers have produced guidelines for test users indicating a range of adjustments to procedures that can be considered. SHL and ASE are just two of those who have done that.

brilliant tip

If you do have special needs, make sure they are known to those responsible for the testing arrangements.

'Respond in your own handwriting'

You may think that the form in which you might make your initial response to a job advertisement has little to do with testing and, if so, you would be in a sense both right and wrong. What you might be getting into is assessment by graphology – handwriting analysis. This is still quite often spoken of in the same breath as testing, but so is astrology, yet it does not comply with any clear testing standards. The BPS for one, which oversees testing in the UK, will have nothing to do with it. Also, if you are dyslexic, as just discussed, you might need more time and this might be in part because you have difficulty with handwriting. Thus any invitation to respond in your own hand could be running foul of professional standards and disability discrimination.

Note that the requirement to make a handwritten application is far less common than it was in the past. Also note that it is unlikely that those who do make such a stipulation, whether intending to use graphology or not, will be aware that they might be doing something wrong. So, you may need to persist in your challenge.

Also note that the use of graphology is by no means confined to initial applications, so you may find yourself asked to produce a sample of your handwriting at some other stage in the selection process. Although not commonly used by British companies it is very popular in France, so if you are applying to the British subsidiary of a French enterprise you may well come across it.

The riddle of culture-fair testing

Sometimes tests are criticised because they appear to be insensitive to people from different cultures and backgrounds who might be taking them. If so they might well be implicated in indirect discrimination. Often, though, criticism is directed at one or two items, involving complaints such as, 'We don't play cricket where I come from, so how can I make a choice between that and basketball?' Such a difficulty with one or two items of that sort would be unlikely to negate the whole of a personality measure, but is representative of the type of comment made.

You might have a different case to pursue once you have had feedback. For example, you might be told that you appear to be far less confrontational than average and 'therefore' will not be effective in negotiation. You might then be inclined to reason that in your culture negotiation is never confrontational but conducted by a slow and diplomatic process. Whether or not the test and the assertion about your lack of confrontation are fair will then depend on whether or not your style of negotiation would be viable in the job in question.

> sometimes tests are criticised because they appear to be insensitive to people from different cultures

Of more concern may be some aspects of the 'stage management' of the whole testing process. For example, a recruiting manager had arranged for their assessment centres to be set up with an evening arrival before a day of tests and exercises. Their reason for this was that they wanted so see how the candidates would behave 'once they have had a few drinks poured down them'. Clearly this would be potentially discriminatory for those – from Muslims to Mormons – who decline alcohol on religious grounds. As the manager themselves was inclined to partake on these occasions, one might also question just how well they were in a position to judge anything!

What about the Data Protection Act?

Candidates sometimes ask for all of the information arising from the tests or assessment centres and refer to the Data Protection Act 1998 as ensuring their right to this information. (The Act allows for a fee to be charged for access to it.) You may do so because you are dissatisfied with something in your testing experience. In other words, you may be thinking of making a complaint, a subject returned to shortly.

But consider if you are successful in obtaining the requested information, whether it will actually tell you anything of value. What you might get is the technical output from one or more tests. Those using it will have gone through specialised training to interpret it, which might last anything from a week to a year, therefore it might convey very little to you. In fact, I have found different legal authorities, where I am unclear on whether the Data Protection Act does ensure this right of access. If you press for the information, you may be given it, but if you are refused, you may wish to seek legal advice.

Something funny happened

The guidelines for testing indicate that candidates should be allowed to work in peace and quiet and without disturbance. There are a few things that most commonly cause disturbance, some of them within and some outside the control of the test administrator. They are supposed to keep a log of the testing session, including noting if anything untoward has happened. To do this the administrator needs to know about it and clearly may not do so if they are not in the testing room at the time, so make sure that if, for instance, a telephone rings in the room, you bring this to their attention. Also, do check that they are intending to note it in the log and not just make sympathetic apologies to you.

In fact, a telephone ringing is one of the more common disturbances and one that you might want to head off by asking the administrator, if there is a phone in the testing room, whether it has been diverted. Also, you may or may not be asked to ensure that your mobile phone is switched off, but whether or not you are asked, make sure that you do so.

If you are taking tests in a room in a regular offices, as opposed to a specialised testing suite at, say, a test publisher, you should reasonably expect that other staff will have been warned in advance to be quiet as a testing session is in progress. This should also be backed up by a notice on the door advising people of the fact. Look out for such signs as, if you are disturbed, their absence may have been a contributing factor. (Of course having signs on the door is not a total guarantee of quiet. Recently a manager had left the open-plan area where they were based so as to have a loud conversation on their mobile phone in a nearby corridor. They thereby spared their open-plan neighbours, but were a nuisance to the candidate taking a test in a room off the corridor. The sign on the door had either not been noticed or was deliberately being ignored.)

> if the disruption seems to be really extreme, enquire if the testing session can be rescheduled

A fire alarm going off seems to be a surprisingly common occurrence. If it is only a trial run you should have been warned about it in advance and so just have the noise to contend with. Disruptive enough as that may be, it is far less so than if an evacuation is necessary, when you may find yourself standing in a draughty car park for half an hour. If the disruption seems to be really extreme then you may want to enquire if the testing session can be rescheduled. Of course this is unlikely to be particularly convenient to you or to the organisation concerned, but it might lead to a fairer result for you.

Other forms of disruption can arise if the administrator fails to follow the administrative instructions properly. For example, you may be asked to make your responses by pencil or pen, but either way you should be given a spare.

What is not known, of course, is the precise effect of any of these disruptions on your performance, but by noting them you are more likely to be given the benefit of the doubt in marginal cases.

Timing

With timed tests you need to know how the time is going. Very often you will be able to consult your own watch and/or the testing room will have a clock prominently displayed. If neither of these is available then ask to borrow a watch or for a clock to be brought in. (An administrator was once obliged to borrow a clock from the kitchen of a hotel where they were holding an assessment centre; the candidates were assisted in their time management, but the lunch was late.)

 **tip**

Make sure you can keep track of the time.

How to complain

If you do think you have reason to complain, then you will be likely to get furthest if you do so rationally rather than emotionally. Shouting at the test administrator or the person giving you feedback will be unlikely to advance your case much. Also, think about what you are complaining about. Was it actually something about the test that was the cause of your complaint or the fact that you were not offered a job? True, if there was something amiss in the test itself or the way that it was handled, then it may have affected your chances adversely. But, if you don't have very firm grounds for complaint about the testing then you may be missing your real target, for instance someone on a final panel who seemed to take a dislike to you.

If something does seem wrong at the time of testing, mention it then and follow it up in writing afterwards. Otherwise it may seem that you are just trying to find excuses for a poor performance. Putting things in writing is in any case a good idea; it helps you marshal your thoughts and gives the other party the best chance of understanding and handling your complaint.

Be careful about how you cite 'expert' sources. A phone call in which a disgruntled candidate claims they were 'speaking to a psychologist, who said that it wasn't right to use that test', will cut little ice. If your friendly psychologist really has a worthwhile expert opinion then they should be encouraged to put that in writing for you to use. The same goes if you are inclined to consult the publisher of a test. Quoting what you have been told, or think you have been told, by a duty consultant responding to what they think you have experienced, leaves room for much confusion. If you can get the publisher to put their support for you in writing then it is likely to carry much more weight with those involved in the testing process.

Also, consider if you should be addressing your complaint to those running the tests or, rather, to the potential employer. If you really do think that the use of the tests have resulted in unfairness to you then start with those responsible for them and escalate your complaint to the employer if you do not get satisfaction. If, on the other hand, you feel that the whole process or some part of it other than the testing is at fault, then go to the employer straightaway.

You may have a legal claim if you think you have been unfairly discriminated against, however, as noted, the law is not clear in relation to data protection here, and in almost every other aspect of the application of testing. Unlike the United States, which has had similar legislation but for longer, and in what appears to be a much more litigious society than the UK, there is little case law to go on. So, if you think you might have a complaint on legal grounds you will need to consult legal experts. Also, remember that the tests are being used to help fair decision making, not to catch out people who belong to one or other particular group. So, do be vigilant, but try not to be paranoid.

 **tip**

If you do complain, do so carefully and rationally.

CHAPTER 9

Psychometrics – what's in, what's out, what's the future?

The scope of applications

In the early days of psychometrics there was considerable emphasis on the use of special techniques for special jobs. Chapter 3 considered tests of mechanical comprehension for instance, and there was a time when batteries of tests with a special focus were commonly used. Many of these were aimed at shop floor jobs with measures including speed of hand–eye co-ordination. With changing patterns of work there has been less emphasis on such measures, though as seen in Chapter 3 again there are tests covering clerical and computer skills which are still quite commonly used.

One development that has been apparent is the application of very specific ability tests for quite senior professional roles. Not all of this is new by any means. The work described in Chapter 1 where tests of manual dexterity were used in the selection of Spacelab scientists is one example. Also, in the selection of pilots, whether civil or military, dynamic tests of tracking ability, for instance, using a joystick to follow a moving spot on a screen, have been in use for many years.

Although scarcely amounting to a groundswell such applications do seem to arise from time to time. Recently a local authority required the use of a test of spatial awareness in a planning job. The authority's area covered a large number of high-rise office blocks and the terrain included a river and a lot of old warehouses. It was argued that there was a real need for the planning manager to be able to visualise that physical environment and the effects of changes to it.

This highly-specialised focus is not just confined to the world of ability testing. A company undertaking operations on North Sea Oil rigs wanted to know which of their specialist technicians would be suitable to promote to supervisor. A personality measure could have been used to look at a range of supervisory inclinations or, indeed, an assessment centre developed in which various elements of their work would be simulated quite closely. In fact research into the role showed that there were a few highly critical areas of supervisory behaviour. One of these was the exercise by the supervisors of 'loose–tight' control. That is, for most of the time they would let the highly-skilled technicians under them function independently. However, they remained alert to serious problems. Some of these could be life-threatening and all of them could be expensive, for instance involving closing down part of the operation. Thus when such an event was anticipated they needed to step in and take direct control. Also, when the danger was past they needed to pull back and let the technicians continue with their normal work. The approach adopted was to develop a structured interview which looked at this characteristic and a handful of others.

Trainability tests

An approach that was current a few years ago was the trainability test. In these tests candidates would be given a series of tasks representing elements of what would be encountered in *training* for the job, rather than the job itself. For example, candidates for jobs as machinists in the garment industry would be given small squares of cloth to stitch on sewing machines. This represented part of the training that they would receive before moving on to make up complete garments. Other roles for which such tests have been devised have been croupiers, for whom the trainability tasks include the calculation of simple bets, and truck drivers given tasks involving driving relatively small vehicles around obstacle courses.

The reason for raising these tests here is to consider them against a background of continuing and increasingly rapid changes in the jobs market. The idea that there are no careers for life any more is scarcely new, but it does seem to have particular significance at present (in the global financial crisis stemming from the credit crunch).

As people change careers and not just jobs it seems likely that there will be a renewed interest in looking at trainability.

In addition to trainability in the sense described above there is an increased interest in a candidate's approach to learning. So, where it is envisaged that people coming into a job are likely to have a lot to learn, both as they start and in relation to the pace of change, employers increasingly want to assess this aspect

> as people change careers and not just jobs there will be a renewed interest in trainability

of candidates' potential. Of the various personality measures referred to in Chapter 4, Wave looks at this quite specifically and both OPQ and 16PF have scales reflecting openness to new ideas. Hence if you are asked to take one of these questionnaires, you may find that there is interest expressed in feedback in your tendency to learn and how you go about it. Something to be aware of, particularly if you are an older candidate, is presenting yourself as knowing it all already and not having any more learning to do.

There are also a number of learning styles instruments available. These look at how people go about learning. Although more often used in connection with development once someone has been employed, they have potential to be used as part of selection. In that context they could help the organisation to see if the learning opportunities that they had set up for a new employee would actually be suitable and, if not, if alternatives could be produced. Thus, if a candidate appeared to like to learn through grasping theory and the only opportunities envisaged were for very practical on-the-job training, this might have an impact on a hiring decision.

What's in and what's out

Every so often a new idea appears in psychometrics, but as in other fields, these ideas usually represent an evolution from something that has gone before. Enthusiastic salespeople of psychometrics claim that their latest product represents a step-function change in test methodology. But very often the tools they are offering represent nothing really new.

One example of a new approach is that of *emotional intelligence*, a concept that emerged in the 1990s and became quickly absorbed into the language of management. It is to do with things such as self-awareness, empathy with others and the controlled application of emotions in interactions with other people. It quickly became captured in a range of psychometric instruments, produced by reputable organisations. I believe these are, however, applied relatively rarely, though the term is still used. The reason why the psychometric aspect has not been more in vogue may lie in the fact that some of what emotional intelligence addresses can be measured by existing personality measures. So, at present, you may find emotional intelligence more likely to be bandied about as a concept than to be asked to take a specific test of it.

Integrity testing – can you trust it to be fair to you?

I was once commissioned to work on the UK version of a short American book on psychometrics, so that it would better fit the market in this country. My main amendment was to cut out a number of references to integrity testing, as such tests are rather rarely used in the UK. They still aren't, but that may change, again with some of the financial shocks in recent years and

> one of the issues with integrity testing is the extent to which it is actually fair to the candidate

currently, from the Enron/Anderson disaster to the current crisis. The essence of integrity testing is to assess matters such as honesty and a value-based stance. Among the approaches used are situational judgement tests as discussed in Chapter 7, with the situations raising issues like conflicts between confidentiality in relation to an individual and the best interests of an organisation.

One of the issues to do with integrity testing is the extent to which it is actually fair to the candidate concerned. There are two aspects of this: does it work and should it be done at all? The first of these was a big concern about the use of the so-called lie detector tests in the USA. These depend upon measuring the so-called galvanic skin response, an increase in sweating on telling a lie, detected by passing a current through the skin. The debate about this raged for many years and the current situation is that such tests are used principally in the field of law enforcement in the USA and a number of other countries, but not widely in the UK. (There was, however, a recent front-page headline in a national newspaper suggesting that lie detection tests might be used to uncover benefit fraud. Of course that does not directly involve a recruitment situation, but it does show that the idea is by no means dead.)

Integrity testing has undoubtedly been successful in some areas and may be increasingly employed. For example in retail there is the problem of 'shrinkage', that is of theft of stock by staff. The use of structured interviews to help eliminate this was pioneered in the USA over 20 years ago. Recently the test publisher Previsor used an online 'conscientiousness' assessment in connection with the hire of retail staff. They report a saving of $78m following its use.

So, if you are a candidate for a job in retail in the future you may well find that you are subject to attempts to assess your integrity. (Interestingly, the dictionary definitions of 'integrity' include 'wholeness' as well as 'honesty'. This is captured in essence in the integrity competency in the 'Professional Skills for Government' model, used by the civil service as part of leadership training. If you are an applicant for a position in the senior civil service you might want to note that it is this latter sense in which the term integrity is used.)

Of course, again in line with the notion that there is nothing new, the various response style indices discussed in Chapter 4 give something of an indication of this. Also, the 'big five' dimension of conscientiousness is generally relevant, as are specific scales with labels including 'principled', 'ethics' and 'honesty' across the range of personality measures. What does seem newer is the increased focus that can be expected in this area.

Clever ways with computers

Everyone can play!

The increasing use of computers in connection with testing, as in so many other fields, seems certain. One test publisher has moved their services almost entirely from paper-based to computer-delivered testing over the last two years. The relative ease with which a series of questions and accompanying computer links can be set up, as opposed to the expense of publishing reams of written material, does of course mean that the barriers to getting into this field are few. This in turn encourages those who have not undertaken the necessary research and development to try their luck and to sell their wares to relatively uninformed employers. It may be difficult for you to know if you are being presented with a 'genuine' psychometric instrument or something that just looks like one. Some of the things to look out for and check are shown in the Brilliant Tips below.

brilliant tips

Identify dubious psychometrics by considering the following:

- Who is the publisher? The names listed in Appendix 1 are reliable and professional, though the list is not exhaustive.
- Does the language used make sense? If not you may be responding to a poorly-translated version developed in a different culture.
- Does the language seem to be American? If so, ask if British norms have been used for the test.
- Is the presentation of what you are expected to do clear?
- Is the test *very* short? If it is then there should be reference to a follow-up of some sort.

One source, many tests

Another piece of computer technology that has been around for some years but is not yet widely applied involves using the power of the computer to generate many tests from a single source. This can be done in two ways. One is to have a large bank of items of equivalent difficulty and then to select randomly from them. The other is for the computer not to store items as such, but just the rule (algorithm) for generating the items. Both of these mean that, for all practical purposes, no two tests are the same, limiting the scope to gain advantage from making multiple applications for the same job – if you didn't get caught by the identity policing (see below) – or somehow making a copy of the test.

Increasingly easy to apply, such techniques are likely to be among the commodities of the test publisher, rather than unique selling points. At present they apply to ability rather than to personality tests, but item banking for the latter seems to be reasonably on the cards. Generation of personality items seems less likely at present.

Follow-ups and response time

Reference to computer produced 'expert' reports with accompanying follow-up questioning was made in Chapter 4. In the future there should be scope for the suggested questions to be more tightly linked to the specific item in the test. This type of detailed examination has not often been available to those interpreting tests and it is very rarely appropriate (for one reason or another) to probe responses at the item level. (Interestingly, the increased use of computers for making and recording response to tests may mean that computer-based probing is the *only* form of probing available to the test user at the item level, as the item details are not always available with computer-generated tests.) The use of probing at this level again suggests no hiding place from the responses that you have made as a candidate. So this particular power of testing adds to methods, such as noting the response times referred to in Chapter 5, to the information on the personality dimensions.

In fact the measurement of response time is a key aspect of an interesting development known as 'Implicit Attitude Theory'. A test based on this theory, published by the firm Hogrefe, can be used to predict the extent to which prejudicial attitudes against a range of sub-groups might lead to discriminatory behaviour. The test sets candidates a sorting task in which positive and negative words are

> a test can be used to predict the extent to which prejudicial attitudes might lead to discriminatory behaviour

associated with pictures of groups against which there might be prejudice. If a candidate is prejudiced against a particular group, then when they are is asked to associate positive words with that group the response time is slower than when the negative words are associated with the same group.

Adaptive testing

Another approach that computers make possible is that of adaptive testing, which is applied in the area of ability assessment. With this approach the difficulty level of the test items varies depending on the responses made. This appears to be a more refined way of realising the concept of maximum performance discussed in Chapter 1. Also, it appears to be in line more with the idea of power testing – giving a definite idea of the ultimate level of mental ability that a candidate can reach.

Computers and assessment centres

The availability of computers makes it relatively simple to run much of an assessment centre on a dispersed basis, rather than gathering the candidates together for the whole of it. At the simplest level this can mean sending an analysis exercise to you, the candidate, as an e-mail attachment, and requiring a response within the normal time limits of the exercise. At present this seems to be done where convenience dictates rather than being standard, but that seems likely to change.

The power of the computer is also increasingly used with in-basket exercises, where all of the items are presented electronically. This gives scope for a dynamic exercise, with e-mails arriving throughout the time involved rather than the candidate dealing with a static pile of paper. It also gives scope for variations on the task, so you are more likely to be asked to indicate priorities and specific actions with this type of delivery. This may help with standardisation of scoring, but does move the task away from a close simulation of handling correspondence.

The technology for video-conferencing has progressively improved in recent years. Thus it is now possible to sit at a table with, say, a couple of other people and for two or three more to appear to be at the other end of the same table, though in reality they might be hundreds of miles away. I don't know of this actually being used for a group discussion exercise, but there is really no reason why it should not be. So you might in future find that you and your fellow candidates are widely dispersed in this type of virtual assessment centre. (The term 'virtual' applying to 'centre': the assessment will be real enough!) For example, a virtual assessment centre has been developed for a major international bank.

Advances in identification

Chapter 5 addressed the question of identifying those who were taking tests. One further advance here is in the use of retinal imaging – using an eye print rather like a fingerprint. Another is through the use of a webcam, common on many computers and likely to be a continuing feature. Many recruitment consultancies have for years been taking photographs of candidates appearing at their offices and the use of the webcam at the testing stage will make it possible to link the two images.

Individuals and teams

Another development which is by no means new, but which seems likely to gather pace, is the use of tests in relation to whole teams, not just individuals. This seems particularly likely to increase in connection with the large number of mergers and reorganisations in hand globally. Thus psychometric measures can

> another development likely to gather pace is the use of tests in relation to whole teams

be used to ensure that there is a balance of ability in a team and to warn of any possible points of friction amongst team members.

Positive psychology – the strengths movement

Much of what has been said in this chapter might be seen as indicating ways in which you, the poor candidate, are likely to undergo ever-more intense scrutiny at the hands of those using psychometric instruments. That idea can be rounded off by referring to the point made in different ways at various stages throughout the book, namely that you just have to be honest. However, there is another relatively recent development that it is worth flagging and that is the positive psychology movement. The central idea is that, rather than seeking to tease out people's limitations, it is better to find out about their real strengths and help them to make use of those. That is, perhaps, a worthwhile end to which psychometrics will increasingly be directed. Put another way, it might be seen as polishing brilliance!

Appendix 1: Further sources of information

The British Psychological Society's testing website is worth looking at. It contains quite a lot of background information about tests, including a useful list of frequently asked questions. It is at www.psychtesting.org.uk.

For a substantial set of practice ability tests look at that produced by the publisher SHL at www.shl.com/shl/en-int/candidate helpline.

Information about specific tests where the title is known can sometimes be found by a Google or other search. For example, this works for the verbal reasoning test, the Watson-Glaser Critical Thinking Appraisal, published by Pearson. Also, go into www.pearsonassess.com for information.

Other leading publishers whose websites contain useful information are Hogrefe – www.hogrefe.co.uk and OPP, www.opp.eu.com.

For further practice material go to www.pearson-books.com/psychometrictests.

Appendix 2:
Expert System Report

This report is reproduced by kind permission of SHL Group Limited.

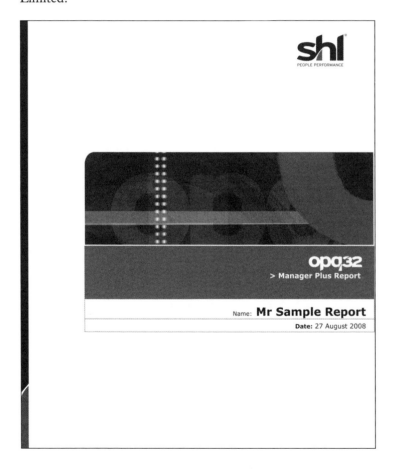

INTRODUCTION

This report is intended for use by line managers and HR professionals. It contains a range of information which is useful to support selection decisions.

It shows:
1. How Mr Report prefers to work (for example whether he likes following rules or is prepared to break them).
2. How Mr Report is likely to interact with his colleagues in a team.
3. His likely performance against a range of competencies proven to be important at work (e.g. Leading & Supervising).

USING THIS REPORT

This report is based on Mr Sample Report's responses to the **Occupational Personality Questionnaire (OPQ)**. His responses have been compared against those of a large relevant comparison group to give a description of Mr Report's preferred approach to work.

The responses Mr Report gave show the way he sees his own behaviour, rather than how another person might describe him. This report describes preferred ways of behaving, rather than actual skills levels. The accuracy of this report depends on the frankness with which he answered the questions as well as his self-awareness. Nevertheless, this report provides important indicators of Mr Report's style at work. This report links the information from the personality questionnaire to the twenty universal competencies.

This report has a shelf-life of 18-24 months and should be treated confidentially. If there are major changes in his life or work he should complete the OPQ again.

If you require support in interpreting this report, please contact a person in your organisation who has received full training in the use of the OPQ.

BEHAVIOUR AT WORK

This section is based on Mr Report's responses to the Occupational Personality Questionnaire (OPQ) and describes his preferred style at work in three key areas: interacting with people, approaching tasks, and managing feelings and emotions.
It concludes with additional comments regarding particularly notable elements of his style.

How is Mr Sample Report likely to interact with people?

- He describes himself as not especially enjoying selling and negotiating
- Has an extreme dislike of taking charge
- Quite prepared to put forward his own opinions or criticise others
- Is inclined to follow his own approach regardless of group consensus
- Very lively and animated in groups
- Likes a balance between spending time alone and spending time with others
- Usually at ease in formal situations or when meeting new people
- Enjoys talking about his own achievements
- Consults others to a moderate degree when making decisions
- Fairly sympathetic and supportive of colleagues

How is Mr Sample Report likely to approach tasks at work?

- Sees himself as having a strong dislike for working with numerical data
- Reports a slight inclination towards taking information or plans proposed to him at face value

---

> 2 Manager Plus Report

© SHL Group Limited 2008

Mr Sample Report: 27 August 2008

- Is slightly more interested than most in the motivations and behaviours of people
- Sees himself as having a definite preference for new ways of working
- He is highly likely to take a theoretical approach enjoying thinking around a problem
- Has a slightly stronger preference than most for coming up with new ideas
- He describes himself as having a marked preference for variety and novelty over routine and repetition in his work
- Has a slight tendency to behave in the same way across different situations and with different people
- Likely to take a strategic view and to think of the longer-term implications
- Shows much less concern for order and detail than most of his peers
- His emphasis on seeing tasks through to completion is slightly lower than most people
- Has a strong tendency to see rules as flexible and feel frustrated by bureaucracy

How are Mr Sample Report's feelings and emotions likely to impact his work?

- He sees himself as relatively free from anxiety or worry in his general work life
- Tends to be as worried and tense as most people before important events
- He sees himself as slightly sensitive to criticism
- Takes a markedly pessimistic view of the future
- Is slightly cautious when judging the reliability and honesty of others
- He describes himself as someone who has a strong tendency to show his emotions openly
- He describes a strong preference for approaching work at a steady pace
- Competition is likely to be of slightly less importance to him than most people
- Describes himself as markedly less ambitious than most
- When making decisions he has a very strong tendency to decide more swiftly than the majority of people

Additional comments about Mr Sample Report's likely behaviour at work:

- Will prefer to take his own approach rather than organising others
- Likes to make swift decisions with an intuitive approach
- Feels frustrated by having to stick to customary methods, rules and procedures

WORKING IN A TEAM

Successful teams share common tasks or projects and work collectively towards the same goals. Within the team each individual makes a specific contribution to the process and thereby affects the success of the team. To achieve their goals the members of a team need to complete a number of key tasks.

Mr Report's likely impact within a team is summarised below. This focuses on his strengths and weaknesses across team tasks.

Overall, Mr Report usually copes better with the tasks related to a project than he does with the people associated with a project.

His strengths are likely to lie in:

- Identifying possible solutions for team tasks
- Building relationships inside and outside the team

He is likely to be as capable as most in:

- Maintaining a positive team climate
- Helping the team to maintain their workload and reach their goals

His weaker areas are likely to lie in:

- Helping the team to evaluate ideas and concepts which contribute to team success
- Steering team activities
- Having an energising impact on other team members
- Planning team work and sustaining team productivity

COMPETENCIES

This section highlights Mr Report's likely performance on key competencies important in the workplace. By selecting those competencies that are most important, and probing those areas for evidence of how he has demonstrated effectiveness, you are more likely to recruit the best person. The competency scores for Mr Report below are based on his responses to the OPQ. Recommended interview questions for each of the competencies are provided in the Universal Competency Framework™ Interview Guide. Competency profiling cards are also available to help in identifying essential or desirable competencies. For more information contact your SHL representative.

Competency	1	2	3	4	5	Important for Success?
Leading and Deciding						
1.1 Deciding & Initiating Action						
1.2 Leading & Supervising						
Supporting and Co-operating						
2.1 Working with People						
2.2 Adhering to Principles and Values [1]						
Interacting and Presenting						
3.1 Relating and Networking						
3.2 Persuading & Influencing						
3.3 Presenting and Communicating Information [2]						
Analysing and Interpreting						
4.1 Writing & Reporting [2]						
4.2 Applying Expertise & Technology [2]						
4.3 Analysing [2]						
Creating and Conceptualising						
5.1 Learning & Researching [2]						
5.2 Creating and Innovating [2]						
5.3 Formulating Strategies and Concepts [2]						
Organising and Executing						
6.1 Planning & Organising						
6.2 Delivering Results & Meeting Customer Expectations [2]						
6.3 Following Instructions & Procedures [2]						
Adapting and Coping						
7.1 Adapting and Responding to change						
7.2 Coping with Pressures & Setbacks						
Enterprising and Performing						
8.1 Achieving Personal Work Goals & Objectives						
8.2 Entrepreneurial & Commercial Thinking [2]						

The index numbers refer to the 20 competency dimensions from the SHL Universal Competency Framework™.

The overall likelihood of Mr Sample Report displaying strength in each competency is shown in the bar graphs in the report.

1	2	3	4	5
Unlikely to be a strength	**Less likely** to be a strength	**Moderately likely** to be a strength	**Quite likely** to be a strength	**Very likely** to be a strength

[1] OPQ32 only assesses some aspects of this competency, specifically related to the areas of rule-following and utilising diversity.
[2] Assessment of this competency could be enhanced by adding a measure of aptitude or ability.

COMPETENCY DEFINITIONS

1. Leading and Deciding

1.1 Deciding and Initiating Action	Takes responsibility for actions, projects and people; takes initiative and works under own direction; initiates and generates activity and introduces changes into work processes; makes quick, clear decisions which may include tough choices or considered risks.
1.2 Leading and Supervising	Provides others with a clear direction; motivates and empowers others; recruits staff of a high calibre; provides staff with development opportunities and coaching; sets appropriate standards of behaviour.

2. Supporting and Co-operating

2.1 Working with People	Shows respect for the views and contributions of other team members; shows empathy; listens, supports and cares for others; consults others and shares information and expertise with them; builds team spirit and reconciles conflict; adapts to the team and fits in well.
2.2 Adhering to Principles and Values	Upholds ethics and values; demonstrates integrity; promotes and defends equal opportunities, builds diverse teams; encourages organisational and individual responsibility towards the community and the environment.

3. Interacting and Presenting

3.1 Relating and Networking	Easily establishes good relationships with customers and staff; relates well to people at all levels; builds wide and effective networks of contacts; uses humour appropriately to bring warmth to relationships with others.
3.2 Persuading and Influencing	Gains clear agreement and commitment from others by persuading, convincing and negotiating; makes effective use of political processes to influence and persuade others; promotes ideas on behalf of oneself or others; makes a strong personal impact on others; takes care to manage one's impression on others.
3.3 Presenting and Communicating Information	Speaks fluently; expresses opinions, information and key points of an argument clearly; makes presentations and undertakes public speaking with skill and confidence; responds quickly to the needs of an audience and to their reactions and feedback; projects credibility.

4. Analysing and Interpreting

4.1 Writing and Reporting	Writes convincingly; writes clearly, succinctly and correctly; avoids the unnecessary use of jargon or complicated language; writes in a well-structured and logical way; structures information to meet the needs and understanding of the intended audience.
4.2 Applying Expertise and Technology	Applies specialist and detailed technical expertise; uses technology to achieve work objectives; develops job knowledge and expertise (theoretical and practical) through continual professional development; demonstrates an understanding of different organisational departments and functions.
4.3 Analysing	Analyses numerical data and all other sources of information, to break them into component parts, patterns and relationships; probes for further information or greater understanding of a problem; makes rational judgements from the available information and analysis; demonstrates an understanding of how one issue may be a part of a much larger system.

5. Creating and Conceptualising

5.1 Learning and Researching	Rapidly learns new tasks and commits information to memory quickly; demonstrates an immediate understanding of newly presented information; gathers comprehensive information to support decision making; encourages an organisational learning approach (i.e. learns from successes and failures and seeks staff and customer feedback).
5.2 Creating and Innovating	Produces new ideas, approaches, or insights; creates innovative products or designs; produces a range of solutions to problems.
5.3 Formulating Strategies and Concepts	Works strategically to realise organisational goals; sets and develops strategies; identifies, develops positive and compelling visions of the organisation's future potential; takes account of a wide range of issues across, and related to, the organisation.

6. Organising and Executing

6.1 Planning and Organising	Sets clearly defined objectives; plans activities and projects well in advance and takes account of possible changing circumstances; identifies and organises resources needed to accomplish tasks; manages time effectively; monitors performance against deadlines and milestones.
6.2 Delivering Results and Meeting Customer Expectations	Focuses on customer needs and satisfaction; sets high standards for quality and quantity; monitors and maintains quality and productivity; works in a systematic, methodical and orderly way; consistently achieves project goals.
6.3 Following Instructions and Procedures	Not challenging authority; follows procedures and policies; keeps to schedules; arrives punctually for work and meetings; demonstrates commitment to the organisation; complies with legal obligations and safety requirements of the role.

7. Adapting and Coping

7.1 Adapting and Responding to change	Adapts to changing circumstances; tolerates ambiguity; accepts new ideas and change initiatives; adapts interpersonal style to suit different people or situations; shows an interest in new experiences.
7.2 Coping with Pressures and Setbacks	Maintains a positive outlook at work; works productively in a pressurised environment; keeps emotions under control during difficult situations; handles criticism well and learns from it; balances the demands of a work life and a personal life.

8. Enterprising and Performing

8.1 Achieving Personal Work Goals and Objectives	Accepts and tackles demanding goals with enthusiasm; works hard and puts in longer hours when it is necessary; seeks progression to roles of increased responsibility and influence; identifies own development needs and makes use of developmental or training opportunities.
8.2 Entrepreneurial and Commercial Thinking	Keeps up to date with competitor information and market trends; identifies business opportunities for the organisation; maintains awareness of developments in the organisational structure and politics; demonstrates financial awareness; controls costs and thinks in terms of profit, loss and added value.

Mr Sample Report: 27 August 2008

ASSESSMENT METHODOLOGY

This Profile is based upon the following sources of information for Mr Sample Report:

Questionnaire / Ability Test	Comparison Group	Used
UK English OPQ32i	OPQ32i Managerial and Professional 2005	Yes

ABOUT THIS REPORT

This report was generated using the SHL Expert Assessment System. It includes information from the Occupational Personality Questionnaire (OPQ32). The use of this questionnaire is limited to those people who have received specialist training in its use and interpretation.

The report herein is generated from the results of a questionnaire answered by the respondent and substantially reflects the answers made by them. Due consideration must be given to the subjective nature of questionnaire-based ratings in the interpretation of this data. This report has been generated electronically – the user of the software can make amendments and additions to the text of the report.

SHL Group Limited and its associated companies cannot guarantee that the contents of this report are the unchanged output of the computer system. We can accept no liability for the consequences of the use of this report and this includes liability of every kind (including negligence) for its contents.

Person Detail Section

Name	Mr Sample Report
Date	27 August 2008
Candidate Data	RP1=4, RP2=2, RP3=7, RP4=8, RP5=9, RP6=6, RP7=7, RP8=3, RP9=5, RP10=7, TS1=2, TS2=4, TS3=7, TS4=3, TS5=9, TS6=7, TS7=8, TS8=4, TS9=8, TS10=3, TS11=4, TS12=3, FE1=7, FE2=5, FE3=4, FE4=3, FE5=4, FE6=3, FE7=3, FE8=4, FE9=4, FE10=9, CNS=5

The Manager Plus Report Version Number: 2.1

Index